Making Strategy Works

ManageMentor Skill Pack

MANAGE ■ MENTOR
BUSINESS MANAGEMENT

Lesson From,

Bob Wolf, Daniel Goleman, John Kotter, Robert Eckert,
Nick Craig, Robert Thomas, John Hamm, Michael
Watkins, David Rooke, Diana Mayer

Copyright © 2015 ManageMentor Business Management.
Nürnberg, Germany.

A CIP catalogue record for this title is available from the British
Library
ISBN: 1515005194

ISBN-13: 978-1515005193

Printed and bound by
Amazon Media EU S.à r.l. , 5 Rue Plaetis, L-2338 Luxemburg.
Amazon.com, Inc.; Seattle, WA 98108-1226, USA

CONTENTS

ACKNOWLEDGMENTS

- *Michael E. Porter* is the Bishop William Lawrence University Professor at Harvard University, based at Harvard Business School in Boston. He is a sixtime McKinsey Award winner, including for his most recent HBR article, "Strategy and Society," coauthored with Mark R. Kramer (December 2006).

- *Gary Hamel* is a visiting professor of strategy and international management at the London Business School in London, England, and chairman of Strategos, an international consulting firm based in Menlo Park, California. He is coauthor, with C.K. Prahalad, of "Competing for the Future" (HBR July-August 1994).

- *Roger L. Martin* is a professor and the former dean at the University of Toronto's Rotman School of Management. He is a coauthor (with A.G. Lafley) of Playing to Win: How Strategy Really Works (Harvard Business Review Press, 2013).

- *Nadim F. Matta* is a senior partner of Robert H. Schaffer & Associates, a management consulting firm based in Stamford, Connecticut. Prior to joining RHS&A, he worked for USAID and then headed the food distribution program for Save the Children during the civil war in Lebanon.

- *Ronald N. Ashkenas* is a managing partner of RHS&A. He has written three previous articles for HBR, most recently "Integration Managers: Special Leaders for Special Times" (with Suzanne C. Francis, November– December 2000).

- *Andrew Campbell* is a director of the Ashridge Strategic Management Centre, an organization based in London that conducts research on the management of multibusiness companies. He is also a visiting professor at City University Business School in London.

- *Marcus Alexander* is also a director of the Ashridge Strategic Management Centre. His research focuses on strategy and on managing beyond an organization's boundaries through alliances, partnership sourcing, and networks.

- *H. Irving Grousbeck* is a consulting professor of management at Stanford Graduate School of Business and a director of its Center for Entrepreneurial Studies.

- *David B. Yoffie* is the Max and Doris Starr Professor of International Business Administration and senior associate dean in charge of executive education at Harvard Business School.

- *Mary Kwak*, in Washington, DC, is a former research associate at Harvard Business School. All information on Intel and Microsoft in this article is based on published HBS case materials and recently released government documents.

- *Fernando Bartolomé* is a professor of management at the Instituto de Empresa Business School in Madrid and an adjunct professor of organizational behavior at Insead in Fontainebleau, France.

CHAPTER 1

What Is Strategy?

I. Operational Effectiveness Is Not Strategy. For almost two decades, managers have been learning to play by a new set of rules. Companies must be flexible to respond rapidly to competitive and market changes. They must benchmark continuously to achieve best practice. They must outsource aggressively to gain efficiencies. And they must nurture a few core competencies in race to stay ahead of rivals.

Positioning—once the heart of strategy—is rejected as too static for today's dynamic markets and changing technologies. According to the new dogma, rivals can quickly copy any market position, and competitive advantage is, at best, temporary.

But those beliefs are dangerous half-truths, and they are leading more and more companies down the path of mutually destructive competition. True, some barriers to competition are falling as regulation eases and markets become global. True, companies have properly invested energy in becoming leaner and more nimble. In many industries, however, what some call *hypercompetition* is a self-inflicted wound, not the inevitable outcome of a changing paradigm of competition.

The root of the problem is the failure to distinguish between operational effectiveness and strategy. The quest for productivity, quality, and speed has spawned a remarkable number of management tools and techniques: total quality management, benchmarking, time-based competition, outsourcing, partnering, reengineering, change management. Although the resulting operational improvements have often been dramatic, many companies have been frustrated by their inability to translate those gains into sustainable profitability. And bit by bit, almost imperceptibly, management tools have taken the place of strategy. As managers push to improve on all fronts, they move farther away from viable competitive positions.

Operational Effectiveness: Necessary but Not Sufficient. Operational effectiveness and strategy are both essential to superior performance, which, after all, is the primary goal of any enterprise. But they work in very different ways.

A company can outperform rivals only if it can establish a difference that it can preserve. It must deliver greater value to customers or create comparable value at a lower cost, or do both. The arithmetic of superior profitability then follows: delivering greater value allows a company to charge higher average unit prices; greater efficiency results in lower average unit costs.

Ultimately, all differences between companies in cost or price derive from the hundreds of activities required to create, produce, sell, and deliver their products or services, such as calling on customers, assembling final products, and training employees. Cost is generated by performing activities, and cost advantage arises from performing particular activities more efficiently than competitors. Similarly, differentiation arises from both the choice of activities and how they are performed. Activities, then are the basic units of competitive advantage. Overall advantage or disadvantage results from all a company's activities, not only a few.

Operational effectiveness (OE) means performing similar activities *better* than rivals perform them. Operational effectiveness includes but is not limited to efficiency. It refers to any number of practices that allow a company to better utilize its inputs by, for example, reducing defects in products or developing better products faster. In contrast, strategic positioning means performing *different* activities from rivals' or performing similar activities in *different* ways.

What Is Strategy?

Differences in operational effectiveness among companies are pervasive. Some companies are able to get more out of their inputs than others because they eliminate wasted effort, employ more advanced technology, motivate employees better, or have greater insight into managing particular activities or sets of activities. Such differences in operational effectiveness are an important source of differences in profitability among competitors because they directly affect relative cost positions and levels of differentiation.

Differences in operational effectiveness were at the heart of the Japanese challenge to Western companies in the 1980s. The Japanese were so far ahead of rivals in operational effectiveness that they could offer lower cost and superior quality at the same time. It is worth dwelling on this point, because so much recent thinking about competition depends on it. Imagine for a moment a *productivity frontier* that constitutes the sum of all existing best practices at any given time. Think of it as the maximum value that a company delivering a particular product or service can create at a given cost, using the best available technologies, skills, management techniques, and purchased inputs. The productivity frontier can apply to individual activities, to groups of linked activities such as order processing and manufacturing, and to an entire company's activities. When a company improves its operational effectiveness, it moves toward the frontier. Doing so may require capital investment, different personnel, or simply new ways of managing.

The productivity frontier is constantly shifting outward as new technologies and management approaches are developed and as new inputs become available. Laptop computers, mobile communications, the Internet, and software such as Lotus Notes, for example, have redefined the productivity frontier for sales-force operations and created rich possibilities for linking sales with such activities as order processing and after-sales support. Similarly, lean production, which involves a family of activities, has allowed substantial improvements in manufacturing productivity and asset utilization.

For at least the past decade, managers have been preoccupied with improving operational effectiveness. Through programs such as TQM, time-based competition, and benchmarking, they have changed how they perform activities in order to eliminate inefficiencies, improve customer satisfaction, and achieve best practice. Hoping to keep up with shifts in the productivity frontier, managers have embraced continuous improvement, empowerment, change management, and the so-called learning organization.

The popularity of outsourcing and the virtual corporation reflect the growing recognition that it is difficult to perform all activities as productively as specialists.

As companies move to the frontier, they can often improve on multiple dimensions of performance at the same time. For example, manufacturers that adopted the Japanese practice of rapid changeovers in the 1980s were able to lower cost and improve differentiation simultaneously. What were once believed to be real trade-offs—between defects and costs, for example—turned out to be illusions created by poor operational effectiveness. Managers have learned to reject such false trade-offs.

Constant improvement in operational effectiveness is necessary to achieve superior profitability. However, it is not usually sufficient. Few companies have competed successfully on the basis of operational effectiveness over an extended period, and staying ahead of rivals gets harder every day. The most obvious reason for that is the rapid diffusion of best practices. Competitors can quickly imitate management techniques, new technologies, input improvements, and superior ways of meeting customers' needs. The most generic solutions—those that can be used in multiple settings—diffuse the fastest. Witness the proliferation of OE techniques accelerated by support from consultants.

OE competition shifts the productivity frontier outward, effectively raising the bar for everyone. But although such competition produces absolute improvement in operational effectiveness, it leads to relative improvement for no one. Consider the $5 billion-plus U.S. commercial-printing industry. The major players—R.R. Donnelley & Sons Company,

Quebecor, World Color Press, and Big Flower Press—are competing head to head, serving all types of customers, offering the same array of printing technologies (gravure and web offset), investing heavily in the same new equipment, running their presses faster, and reducing crew sizes. But the resulting major productivity gains are being captured by customers and equipment suppliers, not retained in superior profitability. Even industry-leader Donnelley's profit margin, consistently higher than 7% in the 1980s, fell to less than 4.6% in 1995. This pattern is playing itself out in industry after industry. Even the Japanese, pioneers of the new competition, suffer from persistently low profits.

The second reason that improved operational effectiveness is insufficient—competitive convergence—is more subtle and insidious. The more benchmarking companies do, the more they look alike. The more that rivals outsource activities to efficient third parties, often the same ones, the more generic those activities become. As rivals imitate one another's improvements in quality, cycle times, or supplier partnerships, strategies converge and competition becomes a series of races down identical paths that no one can win. Competition based on operational effectiveness alone is mutually destructive, leading to wars of attrition that can be arrested only by limiting competition.

The recent wave of industry consolidation through mergers makes sense in the context of OE competition. Driven by performance pressures but lacking strategic vision, company after company has had no better idea than to buy up its rivals. The competitors left standing are often those that outlasted others, not companies with real advantage.

After a decade of impressive gains in operational effectiveness, many companies are facing diminishing returns. Continuous improvement has been etched on managers' brains. But ist tools unwittingly draw companies toward imitation and homogeneity. Gradually, managers have let operational effectiveness supplant strategy. The result is zero-sum competition, static or declining prices, and pressures on costs that compromise companies' ability to invest in the business for the long term.

II. Strategy Rests on Unique Activities. Competitive strategy is about being different. It means deliberately choosing a different set of activities to deliver a unique mix of value.

Southwest Airlines Company, for example, offers short-haul, low-cost, point-to-point service between midsize cities and secondary airports in large cities. Southwest avoids large airports and does not fly great distances. Its customers include business travelers, families, and students. Southwest's frequent departures and low fares attract price-sensitive customers who otherwise would travel by bus or car, and convenience-oriented travelers who would choose a full-service airline on other routes.

Most managers describe strategic positioning in terms of their customers: "Southwest Airlines serves price- and convenience-sensitive travelers," for example. But the essence of strategy is in the activities—choosing to perform activities differently or to perform different activities than rivals. Otherwise, a strategy is nothing more than a marketing slogan that will not withstand competition.

A full-service airline is configured to get passengers from almost any point A to any point B. To reach a large number of destinations and serve passengers with connecting flights, fullservice airlines employ a hub-and-spoke system centered on major airports. To attract passengers who desire more comfort, they offer first-class or business-class service. To accommodate passengers who must change planes, they coordinate schedules and check and transfer baggage. Because some passengers will be traveling for many hours, full-service airlines serve meals.

Southwest, in contrast, tailors all its activities to deliver low-cost, convenient service on its particular type of route. Through fast turnarounds at the gate of only 15 minutes, Southwest is able to keep planes flying longer hours than rivals and provide frequent departures with fewer aircraft. Southwest does not offer meals, assigned seats, interline baggage checking, or premium classes of service. Automated ticketing at the gate encourages customers to bypass travel agents, allowing Southwest to avoid their commissions. A standardized fleet of 737 aircraft boosts the efficiency of maintenance.

Operational Effectiveness Versus Strategic Positioning

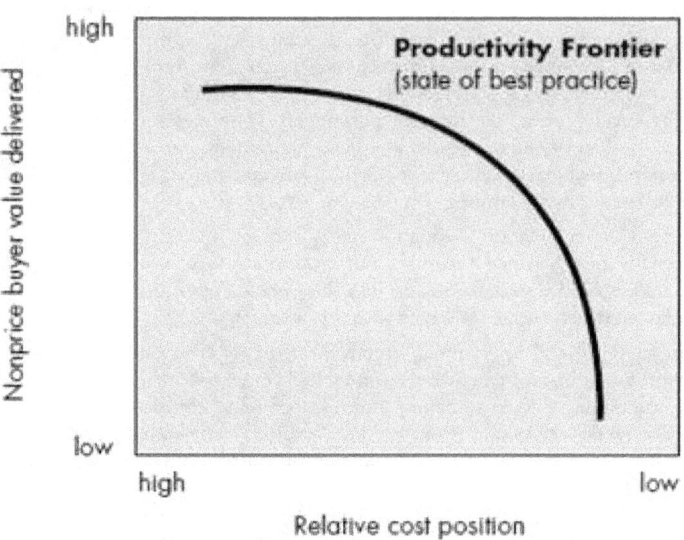

Southwest has staked out a unique and valuable strategic position based on a tailored set of activities. On the routes served by Southwest, a full-service airline could never be as convenient or as low cost. Ikea, the global furniture retailer based in Sweden, also has a clear strategic positioning. Ikea targets young furniture buyers who want style at low cost. What turns this marketing concept into a strategic positioning is the tailored set of activities that make it work. Like Southwest, Ikea has chosen to perform activities differently from its rivals.

Consider the typical furniture store. Showrooms display samples of the merchandise. One area might contain 25 sofas; another will display five dining tables. But those items represent only a fraction of the choices available to customers. Dozens of books displaying fabric swatches or wood samples or alternate styles offer customers thousands of product varieties to choose from. Salespeople often escort customers through the store, answering questions and helping them navigate this maze of choices. Once a customer makes a selection, the order is relayed to a third-party manufacturer. With luck, the furniture will be delivered to the customer's home within six to eight weeks. This is a value chain that maximizes customization and service but does so at high cost.

In contrast, Ikea serves customers who are happy to trade off service for cost. Instead of having a sales associate trail customers around the store, Ikea uses a self-service model based on clear, in-store displays. Rather than rely solely on third-party manufacturers, Ikea designs its own low-cost, modular, ready-to-assemble furniture to fit its positioning. In huge stores, Ikea displays every product it sells in room-like settings, so customers don't need a decorator to help them imagine how to put the pieces together. Adjacent to the furnished showrooms is a warehouse section with the products in boxes on pallets. Customers are expected to do their own pickup and delivery, and Ikea will even sell you a roof rack for your car that you can return for a refund on your next visit.

Although much of its low-cost position comes from having customers "do it themselves," Ikea offers a number of extra services that its competitors do not. In-store child care is one. Extended hours are another. Those services are uniquely aligned with the needs of its customers, who are young, not wealthy, likely to have children (but no nanny), and, because they work for a living, have a need to shop at odd hours.

Japanese Companies Rarely Have Strategies. The Japanese triggered a global revolution in operational effectiveness in the 1970s and 1980s, pioneering practices such as total quality management and continuous improvement. As a result, Japanese manufacturers enjoyed substantial cost and quality advantages for many years.

But Japanese companies rarely developed distinct strategic positions of the kind discussed in this article. Those that did—Sony, Canon, and Sega, for example—were the exception rather than the rule. Most Japanese companies imitate and emulate one another. All rivals offer most if not all product varieties, features, and services; they employ all channels and match one anothers' plant configurations.

The dangers of Japanese-style competition are now becoming easier to recognize. In the 1980s, with rivals operating far from the productivity frontier, it seemed possible to win on both cost and quality indefinitely. Japanese companies were all able to grow in an expanding domestic economy and by penetrating global markets. They appeared unstoppable. But as the gap in operational effectiveness narrows, Japanese companies are increasingly caught in a trap of their own making. If they are to escape the mutually destructive battles now ravaging their performance, Japanese companies will have to learn strategy. To do so, they may have to overcome strong cultural barriers. Japan is notoriously consensus oriented, and companies have a strong tendency to mediate differences among individuals rather than accentuate them. Strategy, on the other hand, requires hard choices. The Japanese also have a deeply ingrained service tradition that predisposes them to go to great lengths to satisfy any need a customer expresses. Companies that compete in that way end up blurring their distinct positioning, becoming all things to all customers.

The Origins of Strategic Positions. Strategic positions emerge from three distinct sources, which are not mutually exclusive and often overlap. First, positioning can be based on producing a subset of an industry's products or services. I call this *variety-based positioning* because it is based on the choice of product or service varieties rather than customer segments. Variety-based positioning makes economic sense when a company can best produce particular products or services using distinctive sets of activities.

Jiffy Lube International, for instance, specializes in automotive lubricants and does not offer other car repair or maintenance services. Its value chain produces faster service at a lower cost than broader line repair shops, a combination so attractive that many customers subdivide their purchases, buying oil changes from the focused competitor, Jiffy Lube, and going to rivals for other services.

The Vanguard Group, a leader in the mutual fund industry, is another example of varietybased positioning. Vanguard provides an array of common stock, bond, and money market funds that offer predictable performance and rock-bottom expenses. The company's investment approach deliberately sacrifices the possibility of extraordinary performance in any one year for good relative performance in every year. Vanguard is known, for example, for its index funds. It avoids making bets on interest rates and steers clear of narrow stock groups. Fund managers keep trading levels low, which holds expenses down; in addition, the company discouragesccustomers from rapid buying and selling becausecdoing so drives up costs and can force acfund manager to trade in order to deploy new capital and raise cash for redemptions.cVanguard also takes a consistent low-cost approachcto managing distribution, customerc service, and marketing. Many investors include one or more Vanguard funds in their portfolio, while buying aggressively managed or specialized funds from competitors.

The people who use Vanguard or Jiffy Lube are responding to a superior value chain for a particular type of service. A variety-based positioning can serve a wide array of customers, but for most it will meet only a subset of their needs.

A second basis for positioning is that of serving most or all the needs of a particular group of customers. I call this *needs-based positioning,* which comes closer to traditional thinking about targeting a segment of customers. It arises when there are groups of customers with differing needs, and when a tailored set of activities can serve those needs best. Some groups of customers are more price sensitive than others, demand different product features, and need varying amounts of information, support, and services. Ikea's customers are a good example of such a group. Ikea seeks to meet all the home furnishing needs of its target customers, not just a subset of them.

A variant of needs-based positioning arises when the same customer has different needs on different occasions or for different types of transactions. The same person, for example, may have different needs when traveling on business than when traveling for pleasure with the family. Buyers of cans—beverage companies, for example—will likely have different needs from their primary supplier than from their secondary source.

It is intuitive for most managers to conceive of their business in terms of the customers' needs they are meeting. But a critical element of needs-based positioning is not at all intuitive and is often overlooked. Differences in needs will not translate into meaningful positions unless the best set of activities to satisfy them *also* differs. If that were not the case, every competitor could meet those same needs, and there would be nothing unique or valuable about the positioning.

In private banking, for example, Bessemer Trust Company targets families with a minimum of $5 million in investable assets who want capital preservation combined with wealth accumulation. By assigning one sophisticated account officer for every 14 families, Bessemer has configured its activities for personalized service. Meetings, for example, are more likely to be held at a client's ranch or yacht than in the office. Bessemer offers a wide array of customized services, including investment management and estate administration, oversight of oil and gas investments, and accounting for racehorses and aircraft. Loans, a staple of most private banks, are rarely needed by Bessemer's clients and make up a tiny fraction of its client balances and income. Despite the most generous compensation of account officers and the highest personnel cost as a percentage of operating expenses, Bessemer's differentiation with its target families produces a return on equity estimated to be the highest of any private banking competitor.

Citibank's private bank, on the other hand, serves clients with minimum assets of about $250,000 who, in contrast to Bessemer's clients, want convenient access to loans—from jumbo mortgages to deal financing. Citibank's account managers are primarily lenders. When clients need other services, their account manager refers them to other Citibank specialists, each of whom handles prepackaged products. Citibank's system is less customized than Bessemer's and allows it to have a lower manager-to-client ratio of 1:125. Biannual office meetings are offered only for the largest clients. Both Bessemer and Citibank have tailored their activities to meet the needs of a different group of private banking customers. The same value chain cannot profitably meet the needs of both groups.

The third basis for positioning is that of segmenting customers who are accessible in different ways. Although their needs are similar to those of other customers, the best configuration of activities to reach them is different. I call this *access-based positioning* . Access can be a function of customer geography or customer scale or of anything that requires a different set of activities to reach customers in the best way.

Segmenting by access is less common and less well understood than the other two bases. Carmike Cinemas, for example, operates movie theaters exclusively in cities and towns with populations under 200,000. How does Carmike make money in markets that are not only small but also won't support big-city ticket prices? It does so through a set of activities that result in a lean cost structure. Carmike's small-town customers can be served through standardized, low-cost theater complexes requiring fewer screens and less sophisticated projection technology than big-city theaters. The company's proprietary information system and management process eliminate the need for local administrative staff beyond a single theater manager. Carmike also reaps advantages from centralized purchasing, lower rent and payroll costs (because of its locations), and rock-bottom corporate overhead of 2% (the industry average is 5%). Operating in small communities also allows Carmike to practice a highly personal form of marketing in which the theater manager knows patrons and promotes attendance through personal contacts. By being the dominant if not the only theater in its markets—the main competition is often the high school football team—Carmike is also able to get its pick of films and negotiate better terms with distributors.

Rural versus urban-based customers are one example of access driving differences in activities. Serving small rather than large customers or densely rather than sparsely situated customers are other examples in which the best way to configure marketing, order processing, logistics, and after-sale service activities to meet the similar needs of distinct groups will often differ.

Positioning is not only about carving out a niche. A position emerging from any of the sources can be broad or narrow. A focused competitor, such as Ikea, targets the special needs of a subset of customers and designs its activities accordingly. Focused competitors thrive on groups of customers who are overserved (and hence overpriced) by more broadly targeted competitors, or underserved (and hence underpriced). A broadly targeted competitor— for example, Vanguard or Delta Air Lines—serves a wide array of customers, performing a set of activities designed to meet their common needs. It ignores or meets only partially the more idiosyncratic needs of particular customer customer groups.

Whatever the basis—variety, needs, access, or some combination of the three—positioning requires a tailored set of activities because it is always a function of differences on the supply side; that is, of differences in activities. However, positioning is not always a function of differences on the demand, or customer, side. Variety and access positionings, in particular, do not rely on *any* customer differences. In practice, however, variety or access differences often accompany needs differences. The tastes—that is, the needs—of Carmike's smalltown customers, for instance, run more toward comedies, Westerns, action films, and family entertainment. Carmike does not run any films rated NC-17.

Having defined positioning, we can now begin to answer the question, "What is strategy?" Strategy is the creation of a unique and valuable position, involving a different set of activities. If there were only one ideal position, there would be no need for strategy. Companies would face a simple imperative—win the race to discover and preempt it. The essence of strategic positioning is to choose activities that are different from rivals'. If the same set of activities were best to produce all varieties, meet all needs, and access all customers, companies could easily shift among them and operational effectiveness would determine performance.

III. A Sustainable Strategic Position Requires Trade-offs. Choosing a unique position, however, is not enough to guarantee a sustainable advantage. A valuable position will attract imitation by incumbents, who are likely to copy it in one of two ways.

First, a competitor can reposition itself to match the superior performer. J.C. Penney, for instance, has been repositioning itself from a Sears clone to a more upscale, fashionoriented, soft-goods retailer. A second and far more common type of imitation is straddling. The straddler seeks to match the benefits of a successful position while maintaining ist existing position. It grafts new features, services, or technologies onto the activities it already performs.

For those who argue that competitors can copy any market position, the airline industry is a perfect test case. It would seem that nearly any competitor could imitate any other airline's activities. Any airline can buy the same planes, lease the gates, and match the menus and ticketing and baggage handling services offered by other airlines.

Continental Airlines saw how well Southwest was doing and decided to straddle. While maintaining its position as a full-service airline, Continental also set out to match Southwest on a number of point-to-point routes. The airline dubbed the new service Continental Lite. It eliminated meals and firstclass service, increased departure frequency, lowered fares, and shortened turnaround time at the gate. Because Continental remained a full-service airline on other routes, it continued to use travel agents and its mixed fleet of planes and to provide baggage checking and seat assignments.

But a strategic position is not sustainable unless there are trade-offs with other positions. Trade-offs occur when activities are incompatible. Simply put, a trade-off means that more of one thing necessitates less of another. An airline can choose to serve meals—adding cost and slowing turnaround time at the gate— or it can choose not to, but it cannot do both without bearing major inefficiencies.

Trade-offs create the need for choice and protect against repositioners and straddlers. Consider Neutrogena soap. Neutrogena Corporation's variety-based positioning is built on a "kind to the skin," residue-free soap formulated for pH balance. With a large detail force calling on dermatologists, Neutrogena's marketing strategy looks more like a drug company's than a soap maker's. It advertises in medical journals, sends direct mail to doctors, attends medical conferences, and performs research at its own Skincare Institute. To reinforce its positioning, Neutrogena originally focused its distribution on drugstores and avoided price promotions. Neutrogena uses a slow, more expensive manufacturing process to mold its fragile soap.

In choosing this position, Neutrogena said no to the deodorants and skin softeners that many customers desire in their soap. It gave up the large-volume potential of selling through supermarkets and using price promotions. It sacrificed manufacturing efficiencies to achieve the soap's desired attributes. In its original positioning, Neutrogena made a whole raft of trade-offs like those, trade-offs that protected the company from imitators.

Trade-offs arise for three reasons. The first is inconsistencies in image or reputation. A company known for delivering one kind of value may lack credibility and confuse customers—or even undermine its reputation—if it delivers another kind of value or attempts to deliver two inconsistent things at the same time. For example, Ivory soap, with its position as a basic, inexpensive everyday soap, would have a hard time reshaping its image to match Neutrogena's premium "medical" reputation. Efforts to create a new image typically cost tens or even hundreds of millions of dollars in a major industry—a powerful barrier to imitation.

Second, and more important, trade-offs arise from activities themselves. Different positions (with their tailored activities) require different product configurations, different equipment, different employee behavior, different skills, and different management systems. Many trade-offs reflect inflexibilities in machinery, people, or systems. The more Ikea has configured its activities to lower costs by having ist customers do their own assembly and delivery, the less able it is to satisfy customers who require higher levels of service.

However, trade-offs can be even more basic. In general, value is destroyed if an activity is overdesigned or underdesigned for its use. For example, even if a given salesperson were capable of providing a high level of assistance to one customer and none to another, the salesperson's talent (and some of his or her cost) would be wasted on the second customer.

Moreover, productivity can improve when variation of an activity is limited. By providing a high level of assistance all the time, the salesperson and the entire sales activity can often achieve efficiencies of learning and scale.

Finally, trade-offs arise from limits on internal coordination and control. By clearly choosing to compete in one way and not another, senior management makes organizational priorities clear. Companies that try to be all things to all customers, in contrast, risk confusion in the trenches as employees attempt to make day-to-day operating decisions without a clear framework.

Positioning trade-offs are pervasive in competition and essential to strategy. They create the need for choice and purposefully limit what a company offers. They deter straddling or repositioning, because competitors that engage in those approaches undermine their strategies and degrade the value of their existing activities.

Trade-offs ultimately grounded Continental Lite. The airline lost hundreds of millions of dollars, and the CEO lost his job. Its planes were delayed leaving congested hub cities or slowed at the gate by baggage transfers. Late flights and cancellations generated a thousand complaints a day. Continental Lite could not afford to compete on price and still pay standard travel-agent commissions, but neither could it do without agents for its full-service business. The airline compromised by cutting commissions for all Continental flights across the board. Similarly, it could not afford to offer the same frequent-flier benefits to travelers paying the much lower ticket prices for Lite service. It compromised again by lowering the rewards of Continental's entire frequent-flier program. The results: angry travel agents and full-service customers.

Continental tried to compete in two ways at once. In trying to be low cost on some routes and full service on others, Continental paid an enormous straddling penalty. If there were no trade-offs between the two positions, Continental could have succeeded. But the absence of trade-offs is a dangerous half-truth that managers must unlearn. Quality is not always free. Southwest's convenience, one kind of high quality, happens to be consistent with low costs because its frequent departures are facilitated by a number of low-cost practices—fast gate turnarounds and automated ticketing, for example. However, other dimensions of airline quality—an assigned seat, a meal, or baggage transfer—require costs to provide.

In general, false trade-offs between cost and quality occur primarily when there is redundant or wasted effort, poor control or accuracy, or weak coordination. Simultaneous improvement of cost and differentiation is possible only when a company begins far behind the productivity frontier or when the frontier shifts outward. At the frontier, where companies have achieved current best practice, the trade-off between cost and differentiation is very real indeed.

After a decade of enjoying productivity advantages, Honda Motor Company and Toyota Motor Corporation recently bumped up against the frontier. In 1995, faced with increasing customer resistance to higher automobile prices, Honda found that the only way to produce a less-expensive car was to skimp on features. In the United States, it replaced the rear disk brakes on the Civic with lowercost drum brakes and used cheaper fabric for the back seat, hoping customers would not notice. Toyota tried to sell a version of its bestselling Corolla in Japan with unpainted bumpers and cheaper seats. In Toyota's case, customers rebelled, and the company quickly dropped the new model.

For the past decade, as managers have improved operational effectiveness greatly, they have internalized the idea that eliminating trade-offs is a good thing. But if there are no trade-offs companies will never achieve a sustainable advantage. They will have to run faster and faster just to stay in place.

As we return to the question, What is strategy? we see that trade-offs add a new dimension to the answer. Strategy is making trade-offs in competing. The essence of strategy is choosing what *not* to do. Without tradeoffs, there would be no need for choice and thus no need for strategy. Any good idea could and would be quickly imitated. Again, performance would once again depend wholly on operational effectiveness.

IV. Fit Drives Both Competitive Advantage and Sustainability. Positioning choices determine not only which activities a company will perform and how it will configure individual activities but also how activities relate to one another. While operational effectiveness is about achieving excellence in individual activities, or functions, strategy is about *combining* activities.

Southwest's rapid gate turnaround, which allows frequent departures and greater use of aircraft, is essential to its high-convenience, low-cost positioning. But how does Southwest achieve it? Part of the answer lies in the com pany's well-paid gate and ground crews, whose productivity in turnarounds is enhanced by flexible union rules. But the bigger part of the answer lies in how Southwest performs other activities. With no meals, no seat assignment, and no interline baggage transfers, Southwest avoids having to perform activities that slow down other airlines. It selects airports and routes to avoid congestion that introduces delays. Southwest's strict limits on the type and length of routes make standardized aircraft possible: every aircraft Southwest turns is a Boeing 737.

What is Southwest's core competence? Ist key success factors? The correct answer is that everything matters. Southwest's strategy involves a whole system of activities, not a collection of parts. Its competitive advantage comes from the way its activities fit and reinforce one another.

Fit locks out imitators by creating a chain that is as strong as its *strongest* link. As in most companies with good strategies, Southwest's activities complement one another in ways that create real economic value. One activity's cost, for example, is lowered because of the way other activities are performed. Similarly, one activity's value to customers can be enhanced by a company's other activities. That is the way strategic fit creates competitive advantage and superior profitability.

Types of Fit. The importance of fit among functional policies is one of the oldest ideas in strategy. Gradually, however, it has been supplanted on the management agenda. Rather than seeing the company as a whole, managers have turned to "core" competencies, "critical" resources, and "key" success factors. In fact, fit is a far more central component of competitive advantage than most realize.

Fit is important because discrete activities often affect one another. A sophisticated sales force, for example, confers a greater advantage when the company's product embodies premium technology and its marketing approach emphasizes customer assistance and support. A production line with high levels of model variety is more valuable when combined with an inventory and order processing system that minimizes the need for stocking finished goods, a sales process equipped to explain and encourage customization, and an advertising theme that stresses the benefits of product variations that meet a customer's special needs. Such complementarities are pervasive in strategy. Although some fit among activities is generic and applies to many companies, the most valuable fit is strategy-specific because it enhances a position's uniqueness and amplifies trade-offs.

There are three types of fit, although they are not mutually exclusive. First-order fit is *simple consistency* between each activity (function) and the overall strategy. Vanguard, for example, aligns all activities with its low-cost strategy. It minimizes portfolio turnover and does not need highly compensated money managers. The company distributes its funds directly, avoiding commissions to brokers. It also limits advertising, relying instead on public relations and word-of-mouth recommendations. Vanguard ties its employees' bonuses to cost savings.

Consistency ensures that the competitive advantages of activities cumulate and do not erode or cancel themselves out. It makes the strategy easier to communicate to customers, employees, and shareholders, and improves implementation through single-mindedness in the corporation.

Second-order fit occurs when *activities are reinforcing* . Neutrogena, for example, markets to upscale hotels eager to offer their guests a soap recommended by dermatologists. Hotels grant Neutrogena the privilege of using its customary packaging while requiring other soaps to feature the hotel's name. Once guests have tried Neutrogena in a luxury hotel, they are more likely to purchase it at the drugstore or ask their doctor about it. Thus Neutrogena's medical and hotel marketing activities reinforce one another, lowering total marketing costs.

In another example, Bic Corporation sells a narrow line of standard, low-priced pens to virtually all major customer markets (retail, commercial, promotional, and giveaway) through virtually all available channels. As with any variety-based positioning serving a broad group of customers, Bic emphasizes a common need (low price for an acceptable pen) and uses marketing approaches with a broad reach (a large sales force and heavy television advertising). Bic gains the benefits of consistency across nearly all activities, including product design that emphasizes ease of manufacturing, plants configured for low cost, aggressive purchasing to minimize material costs, and in-house parts production whenever the economics dictate. Yet Bic goes beyond simple consistency because its activities are reinforcing. For example, the company uses point-of-sale displays and frequent packaging changes to stimulate impulse buying. To handle point-of-sale tasks, a company needs a large sales force. Bic's is the largest in its industry, and it handles point-ofsale activities better than its rivals do. Moreover, the combination of point-of-sale activity, heavy television advertising, and packaging changes yields far more impulse buying than any activity in isolation could.

Third-order fit goes beyond activity reinforcement to what I call *optimization of effort* . The Gap, a retailer of casual clothes, considers product availability in its stores a critical element of its strategy. The Gap could keep products either by holding store inventory or by restocking from warehouses. The Gap has optimized its effort across these activities by restocking its selection of basic clothing almost daily out of three warehouses, thereby minimizing the need to carry large in-store inventories. The emphasis is on restocking because the Gap's merchandising strategy sticks to basic items in relatively few colors. While comparable retailers achieve turns of three to four times per year, the Gap turns its inventory seven and a half times per year. Rapid restocking, moreover, reduces the cost of implementing the Gap's short model cycle, which is six to eight weeks long.

Coordination and information exchange across activities to eliminate redundancy and minimize wasted effort are the most basic types of effort optimization. But there are higher levels as well. Product design choices, for example, can eliminate the need for aftersale service or make it possible for customers to perform service activities themselves. Similarly, coordination with suppliers or distribution channels can eliminate the need for some in-house activities, such as end-user training.

In all three types of fit, the whole matters more than any individual part. Competitive advantage grows out of the *entire system* of activities. The fit among activities substantially reduces cost or increases differentiation. Beyond that, the competitive value of individual activities—or the associated skills, competencies, or resources—cannot be decoupled from the system or the strategy. Thus in competitive companies it can be misleading to explain success by specifying individual strengths, core competencies, or critical resources. The list of strengths cuts across many functions, and one strength blends into others. It is more useful to think in terms of themes that pervade many activities, such as low cost, a particular notion of customer service, or a particular conception of the value delivered. These themes are embodied in nests of tightly linked activities.

Fit and sustainability. Strategic fit among many activities is fundamental not only to competitive advantage but also to the sustainability of that advantage. It is harder for a rival

11

to match an array of interlocked activities than it is merely to imitate a particular sales-force approach, match a process technology, or replicate a set of product features. Positions built on systems of activities are far more sustainable than those built on individual activities.

Consider this simple exercise. The probabil ity that competitors can match any activity is often less than one. The probabilities then quickly compound to make matching the entire system highly unlikely (.9 x .9 = .81; .9 x .9 x .9 x .9 = .66, and so on). Existing companies that try to reposition or straddle will be forced to reconfigure many activities. And even new entrants, though they do not confront the trade-offs facing established rivals, still face formidable barriers to imitation.

The more a company's positioning rests on activity systems with second- and third-order fit, the more sustainable its advantage will be. Such systems, by their very nature, are usually difficult to untangle from outside the company and therefore hard to imitate. And even if rivals can identify the relevant interconnections, they will have difficulty replicating them. Achieving fit is difficult because it requires the integration of decisions and actions across many independent subunits.

A competitor seeking to match an activity system gains little by imitating only some activities and not matching the whole. Performance does not improve; it can decline. Recall Continental Lite's disastrous attempt to imitate Southwest.

Finally, fit among a company's activities creates pressures and incentives to improve operational effectiveness, which makes imitation even harder. Fit means that poor performance in one activity will degrade the performance in others, so that weaknesses are exposed and more prone to get attention. Conversely, improvements in one activity will pay dividends in others. Companies with strong fit among their activities are rarely inviting targets. Their superiority in strategy and in execution only compounds their advantages and raises the hurdle for imitators.

When activities complement one another, rivals will get little benefit from imitation unless they successfully match the whole system. Such situations tend to promote winner-takeall competition. The company that builds the best activity system—Toys R Us, for instance—wins, while rivals with similar strategies—Child World and Lionel Leisure—fall behind. Thus finding a new strategic position is often preferable to being the second or third imitator of an occupied position.

The most viable positions are those whose activity systems are incompatible because of tradeoffs. Strategic positioning sets the tradeoff rules that define how individual activities will be configured and integrated. Seeing strategy in terms of activity systems only makes it clearer why organizational structure, systems, and processes need to be strategy-specific. Tailoring organization to strategy, in turn, makes complementarities more achievable and contributes to sustainability.

One implication is that strategic positions should have a horizon of a decade or more, not of a single planning cycle. Continuity fosters improvements in individual activities and the fit across activities, allowing an organization to build unique capabilities and skills tailored to its strategy. Continuity also reinforces a company's identity.

Conversely, frequent shifts in positioning are costly. Not only must a company reconfigure individual activities, but it must also realign entire systems. Some activities may never catch up to the vacillating strategy. The inevitable result of frequent shifts in strategy, or of failure to choose a distinct position in the first place, is "me-too" or hedged activity configurations, inconsistencies across functions, and organizational dissonance.

What is strategy? We can now complete the answer to this question. Strategy is creating fit among a company's activities. The success of a strategy depends on doing many things well—not just a few—and integrating among them. If there is no fit among activities, there is no distinctive strategy and little sustainability. Management reverts to the simpler task of overseeing independent functions, and operational effectiveness determines an organization's relative performance.

V. Rediscovering StrategyThe Failure to Choose. Why do so many companies fail to have a strategy? Why do managers avoid making strategic choices? Or, having made them in the past, why do managers so often let strategies decay and blur?

Commonly, the threats to strategy are seen to emanate from outside a company because of changes in technology or the behavior of competitors. Although external changes can be the problem, the greater threat to strategy often comes from within. A sound strategy is undermined by a misguided view of competition, by organizational failures, and, especially, by the desire to grow.

Managers have become confused about the necessity of making choices. When many companies operate far from the productivity frontier, trade-offs appear unnecessary. It can seem that a well-run company should be able to beat its ineffective rivals on all dimensions simultaneously. Taught by popular management thinkers that they do not have to make tradeoffs, managers have acquired a macho sense that to do so is a sign of weakness.

Unnerved by forecasts of hypercompetition, managers increase its likelihood by imitating everything about their competitors. Exhorted to think in terms of revolution, managers chase every new technology for its own sake.

The pursuit of operational effectiveness is seductive because it is concrete and actionable. Over the past decade, managers have been under increasing pressure to deliver tangible, measurable performance improvements. Programs in operational effectiveness produce re assuring progress, although superior profitability may remain elusive. Business publications and consultants flood the market with information about what other companies are doing, reinforcing the best-practice mentality. Caught up in the race for operational effectiveness, many managers simply do not understand the need to have a strategy.

Companies avoid or blur strategic choices for other reasons as well. Conventional wisdom within an industry is often strong, homogenizing competition. Some managers mistake "customer focus" to mean they must serve all customer needs or respond to every request from distribution channels. Others cite the desire to preserve flexibility.

Organizational realities also work against strategy. Trade-offs are frightening, and making no choice is sometimes preferred to risking blame for a bad choice. Companies imitate one another in a type of herd behavior, each assuming rivals know something they do not. Newly empowered employees, who are urged to seek every possible source of improvement, often lack a vision of the whole and the perspective to recognize trade-offs. The failure to choose sometimes comes down to the reluctance to disappoint valued managers or employees.

The Growth Trap. Among all other influences, the desire to grow has perhaps the most perverse effect on strategy. Trade-offs and limits appear to constrain growth. Serving one group of customers and excluding others, for instance, places a real or imagined limit on revenue growth. Broadly targeted strategies emphasizing low price result in lost sales with customers sensitive to features or service. Differentiators lose sales to price-sensitive customers.

Managers are constantly tempted to take incremental steps that surpass those limits but blur a company's strategic position. Eventually, pressures to grow or apparent saturation of the target market lead managers to broaden the position by extending product lines, adding new features, imitating competitors' popular services, matching processes, and even making acquisitions. For years, Maytag Corporation's success was based on its focus on reliable, durable washers and dryers, later extended to include dishwashers. However, conventional wisdom emerging within the industry supported the notion of selling a full line of products. Con cerned with slow industry growth and competition from broad-line appliance makers, Maytag was pressured by dealers and encouraged by customers to extend its line. Maytag expanded into refrigerators and cooking products under the Maytag brand and acquired other brands—Jenn-Air, Hardwick Stove, Hoover, Admiral, and Magic Chef—with disparate positions. Maytag has grown substantially from $684 million in 1985 to a peak of $3.4 billion in 1994, but return on sales has declined from 8% to 12% in the 1970s and 1980s to an average of less than 1% between 1989 and 1995. Cost cutting will improve this performance, but laundry and dishwasher products still anchor Maytag's profitability.

Neutrogena may have fallen into the same trap. In the early 1990s, its U.S. distribution broadened to include mass merchandisers such as Wal-Mart Stores. Under the Neutrogena name, the company expanded into a wide variety of products—eye-makeup remover and shampoo, for example—in which it was not unique and which diluted its image, and it began turning to price promotions.

Compromises and inconsistencies in the pursuit of growth will erode the competitive advantage a company had with its original varieties or target customers. Attempts to compete in several ways at once create confusion and undermine organizational motivation and focus. Profits fall, but more revenue is seen as the answer. Managers are unable to make choices, so the company embarks on a new round of broadening and compromises. Often, rivals continue to match each other until desperation breaks the cycle, resulting in a merger or downsizing to the original positioning.

Profitable Growth. Many companies, after a decade of restructuring and cost-cutting, are turning their attention to growth. Too often, efforts to grow blur uniqueness, create compromises, reduce fit, and ultimately undermine competitive advantage. In fact, the growth imperative is hazardous to strategy.

What approaches to growth preserve and reinforce strategy? Broadly, the prescription is to concentrate on deepening a strategic position rather than broadening and compromising it. One approach is to look for extensions of the strategy that leverage the existing activity system by offering features or services that rivals would find impossible or costly to match on a stand-alone basis. In other words, managers can ask themselves which activities, features, or forms of competition are feasible or less costly to them because of complementary activities that their company performs.

Deepening a position involves making the company's activities more distinctive, strengthening fit, and communicating the strategy better to those customers who should value it. But many companies succumb to the temptation to chase "easy" growth by adding hot features, products, or services without screening them or adapting them to their strategy. Or they target new customers or markets in which the company has little special to offer. A company can often grow faster—and far more profitably—by better penetrating needs and varieties where it is distinctive than by slugging it out in potentially higher growth arenas in which the company lacks uniqueness. Carmike, now the largest theater chain in the United States, owes its rapid growth to its disciplined concentration on small markets. The company quickly sells any big-city theaters that come to it as part of an acquisition.

Globalization often allows growth that is consistent with strategy, opening up larger markets for a focused strategy. Unlike broadening domestically, expanding globally is likely to leverage and reinforce a company's unique position and identity.

Companies seeking growth through broadening within their industry can best contain the risks to strategy by creating stand-alone units, each with its own brand name and tailored activities. Maytag has clearly struggled with this issue. On the one hand, it has organized its premium and value brands into separate units with different strategic positions. On the other, it has created an umbrella appliance company for all its brands to gain critical mass. With shared design, manufacturing, distribution, and customer service, it will be hard to avoid homogenization. If a given business unit attempts to compete with different positions for different products or customers, avoiding compromise is nearly impossible.

What Is Strategy?

The Role of Leadership. The challenge of developing or reestablishing a clear strategy is often primarily an organizational one and depends on leadership. With so many forces at work against making choices and tradeoffs in organizations, a clear intellectual framework to guide strategy is a necessary counterweight. Moreover, strong leaders willing to make choices are essential.

In many companies, leadership has degenerated into orchestrating operational improvements and making deals. But the leader's role is broader and far more important. General management is more than the stewardship of individual functions. Its core is strategy: defining and communicating the company's unique position, making trade-offs, and forging fit among activities. The leader must provide the discipline to decide which industry changes and customer needs the company will respond to, while avoiding organizational distractions and maintaining the company'sdistinctiveness. Managers at lower levels lack the perspective and the confidence to maintain a strategy. There will be constant pressures to compromise, relax trade-offs, and emulate rivals. One of the leader's jobs is to teach others in the organization about strategy—and to say no.

Strategy renders choices about what not to do as important as choices about what to do. Indeed, setting limits is another function of leadership. Deciding which target group of customers, varieties, and needs the company should serve is fundamental to developing a strategy. But so is deciding not to serve other customers or needs and not to offer certain features or services. Thus strategy requires constant discipline and clear communication. Indeed, one of the most important functions of an explicit, communicated strategy is to guide employees in making choices that arise because of trade-offs in their individual activities and in day-to-day decisions.

Improving operational effectiveness is a necessary part of management, but it is *not* strategy.

In confusing the two, managers have unintentionally backed into a way of thinking about competition that is driving many industries toward competitive convergence, which is in no one's best interest and is not inevitable.

Managers must clearly distinguish operational effectiveness from strategy. Both are essential, but the two agendas are different.

The operational agenda involves continual improvement everywhere there are no tradeoffs. Failure to do this creates vulnerability even for companies with a good strategy. The operational agenda is the proper place for constant change, flexibility, and relentless efforts to achieve best practice. In contrast, the strategic agenda is the right place for defining a unique position, making clear trade-offs, and tightening fit. It involves the continual search for ways to reinforce and extend the company's position. The strategic agenda demands discipline and continuity; its enemies are distraction and compromise.

Strategic continuity does not imply a static view of competition. A company must continually improve its operational effectiveness and actively try to shift the productivity frontier; at the same time, there needs to be ongoing effort to extend its uniqueness while strengthening the fit among its activities. Strategic continuity, in fact, should make an organization's continual improvement more effective.

A company may have to change its strategy if there are major structural changes in its industry. In fact, new strategic positions often arise because of industry changes, and new entrants unencumbered by history often can exploit them more easily. However, a company's choice of a new position must be driven by the ability to find new trade-offs and leverage a new system of complemen tary activities into a sustainable advantage.

Mapping Activity Systems. Activity-system maps, such as this one for Ikea, show how a company's strategic position is contained in a set of tailored activities designed to deliver it. In companies with a clear strategic position, a number of higher-order strategic themes (in dark grey) can be identified and implemented through clusters of tightly linked activities (in light grey).

Vanguard's Activity System. Activity-system maps can be useful for examining and strengthening strategic fit. A set of basic questions should guide the process. First, is each activity consistent with the overall positioning – the varieties produced, the needs served, and the type of customers accessed? Ask those responsible for each activity to identify how other activities within the company improve or detract from their performance. Second, are there ways to strengthen how activities and groups of activities reinforce one another? Finally, could changes in one activity eliminate the need to perform others?

Southwest Airlines' Activity System

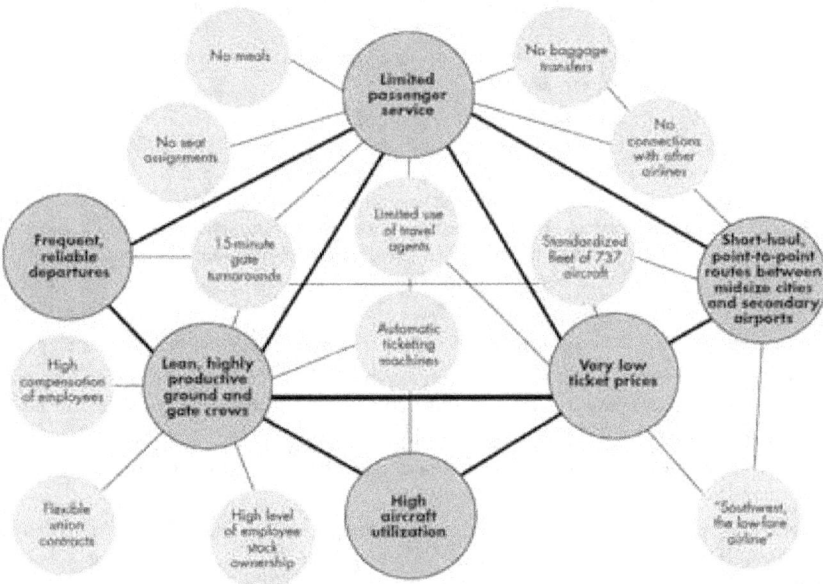

Alternative Views of Strategy The Implicit Strategy Model of the Past Decade

- One ideal competitive position in the industry
- Benchmarking of all activities and achieving best practice
- Aggressive outsourcing and partnering to gain efficiencies
- Advantages rest on a few key success factors, critical resources, core competencies
- Flexibility and rapid responses to all competitive and market changes

Sustainable Competitive Advantage

- Unique competitive position for the company
- Activities tailored to strategy
- Clear trade-offs and choices vis-à-vis competitors
- Competitive advantage arises from fit across activities
- Sustainability comes from the activity system, not the parts

- Operational effectiveness a given

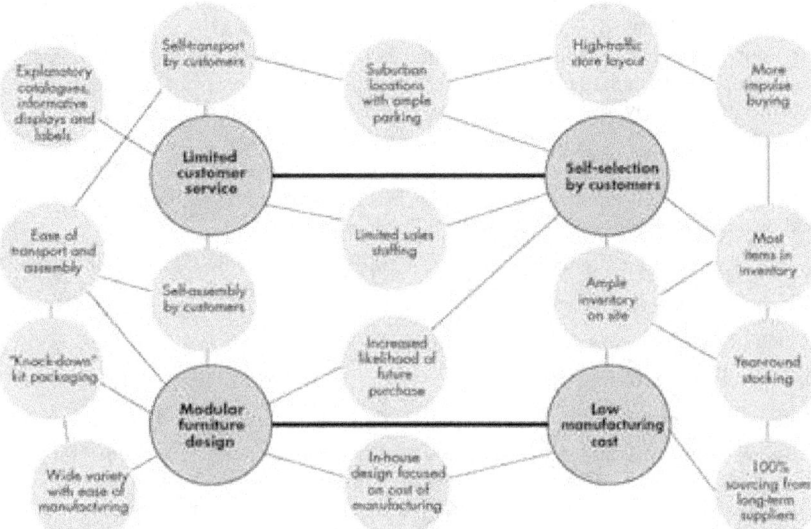

Mapping Activity Systems

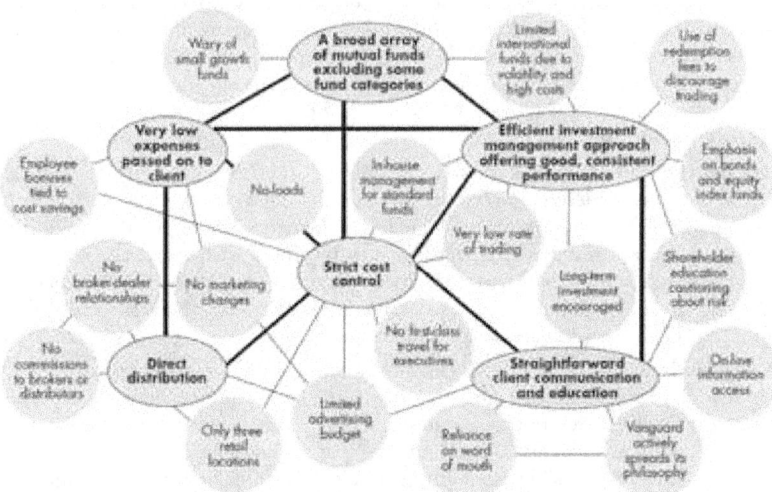

Vanguard's Activity System

Reconnecting with Strategy. Most companies owe their initial success to a unique strategic position involving clear trade-offs. Activities once were aligned with that position. The passage of time and the pressures of growth, however, led to compromises that were, at first, almost imperceptible. Through a succession of incremental changes that each seemed sensible at the time, many established companies have compromised their way to homogeneity with their rivals.

The issue here is not with the companies whose historical position is no longer viable; their challenge is to start over, just as a new entrant would. At issue is a far more common phenomenon: the established company achieving mediocre returns and lacking a clear strategy. Through incremental additions of product varieties, incremental efforts to serve new customer groups, and emulation of rivals' activities, the existing company loses its clear competitive position. Typically, the company has matched many of its competitors' offerings and practices and attempts to sell to most customer groups.

A number of approaches can help a company reconnect with strategy. The first is a careful look at what it already does. Within most well-established companies is a core of uniqueness. It is identified by answering questions such as the following:

- Which of our product or service varieties are the most distinctive?
- Which of our product or service varieties are the most profitable?
- Which of our customers are the most satisfied?
- Which customers, channels, or purchase occasions are the most profitable?
- Which of the activities in our value chain are the most different and effective?

Around this core of uniqueness are encrustations added incrementally over time. Like barnacles, they must be removed to reveal the underlying strategic positioning. A small percentage of varieties or customers may well account for most of a company's sales and especially its profits. The challenge, then, is to refocus on the unique core and realign the company's activities with it. Customers and product varieties at the periphery can be sold or allowed through inattention or price increases to fade away.

A company's history can also be instructive. What was the vision of the founder? What were the products and customers that made the company? Looking backward, one can reexamine the original strategy to see if it is still valid. Can the historical positioning be implemented in a modern way, one consistent with today's technologies and practices? This sort of thinking may lead to a commitment to renew the strategy and may challenge the organization to recover its distinctiveness. Such a challenge can be galvanizing and can instill the confidence to make the needed trade-offs.

Emerging Industries and Technologies. Developing a strategy in a newly emerging industry or in a business undergoing revolutionary technological changes is a daunting proposition. In such cases, managers face a high level of uncertainty about the needs of customers, the products and services that will prove to be the most desired, and the best configuration of activities and technologies to deliver them. Because of all this uncertainty, imitation and hedging are rampant: unable to risk being wrong or left behind, companies match all features, offer all new services, and explore all technologies.

During such periods in an industry's development, its basic productivity frontier is being established or reestablished. Explosive growth can make such times profitable for many companies, but profits will be temporary because imitation and strategic convergence will ultimately destroy industry profitability. The companies that are enduringly successful will be those that begin as early as possible to define and embody in their activities a unique competitive position. A period of imitation may be inevitable in emerging industries, but that period reflects the level of uncertainty rather than a desired state of affairs.

In high-tech industries, this imitation phase often continues much longer than it should. Enraptured by technological change itself, companies pack more features—most of which are never used—into their products while slashing prices across the board. Rarely are trade-offs even considered. The drive for growth to satisfy market pressures leads companies into every product area. Although a few companies with fundamental advantages prosper, the majority are doomed to a rat race no one can win.

Ironically, the popular business press, focused on hot, emerging industries, is prone to presenting these special cases as proof that we have entered a new era of competition in which none of the old rules are valid. In fact, the opposite is true.

Finding New Positions: The Entrepreneurial Edge. Strategic competition can be thought of as the process of perceiving new positions that woo customers from established positions or draw new customers into the market. For example, superstores offering depth of merchandise in a single product category take market share from broad-line department stores offering a more limited selection in many categories. Mail-order catalogs pick off customers who crave convenience. In principle, incumbents and entrepreneurs face the same challenges in finding new strategic positions. In practice, new entrants often have the edge.

Strategic positionings are often not obvious, and finding them requires creativity and insight. New entrants often discover unique positions that have been available but simply overlooked by established competitors. Ikea, for example, recognized a customer group that had been ignored or served poorly. Circuit City Stores' entry into used cars, CarMax, is based on a new way of performing activities—extensive refurbishing of cars, product guarantees, no-haggle pricing, sophisticated use of inhouse customer financing—that has long been open to incumbents.

New entrants can prosper by occupying a position that a competitor once held but has ceded through years of imitation and straddling. And entrants coming from other industries can create new positions because of distinctive activities drawn from their other businesses. CarMax borrows heavily from Circuit City's expertise in inventory management, credit, and other activities in consumer electronics retailing.

Most commonly, however, new positions open up because of change. New customer groups or purchase occasions arise; new needs emerge as societies evolve; new distribution channels appear; new technologies are developed; new machinery or information systems become available. When such changes happen, new entrants, unencumbered by a long history in the industry, can often more easily perceive the potential for a new way of competing. Unlike incumbents, newcomers can be more flexible because they face no trade-offs with their existing activities.

The Idea in Brief

The myriad activities that go into creating, producing, selling, and delivering a product or service are the basic units of competitive advantage.

Operational effectiveness

means performing these activities better—that is, faster, or with fewer inputs and defects—than rivals. Companies can reap enormous advantages from operational effectiveness, as Japanese firms demonstrated in the 1970s and 1980s with such practices as total quality management and continuous improvement. But from a competitive standpoint, the problem with operational effectiveness is that best practices are easily emulated. As all competitors in an industry adopt them, the **productivity frontier**—the maximum value a company can deliver at a given cost, given the best available technology, skills, and management techniques—shifts outward, lowering costs and improving value at the same time. Such competition produces absolute improvement in operational effectiveness, but relative improvement for no one. And the more benchmarking that companies do, the more **competitive convergence** you have—that is, the more indistinguishable companies are from one another.

What Is Strategy?

Strategic positioning attempts to achieve sustainable competitive advantage by preserving what is distinctive about a company. It means performing *different* activities from rivals, or performing *similar* activities in different ways.

Three key principles underlie strategic positioning.

1. Strategy is the creation of a unique and valuable position, involving a different set of activities. Strategic position emerges from three distinct sources:

- serving few needs of many customers (Jiffy Lube provides only auto lubricants)

- serving broad needs of few customers (Bessemer Trust targets only very highwealth clients)

- serving broad needs of many customers in a narrow market (Carmike Cinemas operates only in cities with a population under 200,000)

2. Strategy requires you to make trade-offs in competing—to choose what *not* to do.

Some competitive activities are incompatible; thus, gains in one area can be achieved only at the expense of another area. For example, Neutrogena soap is positioned more as a medicinal product than as a cleansing agent. The company says "no" to sales based on deodorizing, gives up large volume, and sacrifices manufacturing efficiencies. By contrast, Maytag's decision to extend its product line and acquire other brands represented a failure to make difficult trade-offs: the boost in revenues came at the expense of return on sales.

3. Strategy involves creating "fit" among a company's activities.

Fit has to do with the ways a company's activities interact and reinforce one another. For example, Vanguard Group aligns all of its activities with a low-cost strategy; it distributes funds directly to consumers and minimizes portfolio turnover. Fit drives both competitive advantage and sustainability: when activities mutually reinforce each other, competitors can't easily imitate them. When Continental Lite tried to match a few of Southwest Airlines' activities, but not the whole interlocking system, the results were disastrous.

Employees need guidance about how to deepen a strategic position rather than broaden or compromise it. About how to extend the company's uniqueness while strengthening the fit among its activities. This work of deciding which target group of customers and needs to serve requires discipline, the ability to set limits, and forthright communication. Clearly, strategy and leadership are inextricably linked.

CHAPTER 2

The Five Competitive Forces That Shape Strategy

Awareness of the five forces can help a company understand the structure of ist industry and stake out a position that is more profitable and less vulnerable to attack. by Michael E. Porter

In essence, the job of the strategist is to understand and cope with competition. Often, however, managers define competition too narrowly, as if it occurred only among today's direct competitors. Yet competition for profits goes beyond established industry rivals to include four other competitive forces as well: customers, suppliers, potential entrants, and substitute products. The extended rivalry that results from all five forces defines an industry's structure and shapes the nature of competitive interaction within an industry. As different from one another as industries might appear on the surface, the underlying drivers of profitability are the same. The global auto industry, for instance, appears to have nothing in common with the worldwide market for art masterpieces or the heavily regulated health-care delivery industry in Europe. But to understand industry competition and profitability in each of those three cases, one must analyze the industry's underlying structure in terms of the five forces.

If the forces are intense, as they are in such industries as airlines, textiles, and hotels, almost no company earns attractive returns on investment. If the forces are benign, as they are in industries such as software, soft drinks, and toiletries, many companies are profitable. Industry structure drives competition and profitability, not whether an industry produces a product or service, is emerging or mature, high tech or low tech, regulated or unregulated. While a myriad of factors can affect industry profitability in the short run including the weather and the business cycle—industry structure, manifested in the competitive forces, sets industry profitability in the medium and long run.

Understanding the competitive forces, and their underlying causes, reveals the roots of an industry's current profitability while providing a framework for anticipating and influencing competition (and profitability) over time. A healthy industry structure should be as much a competitive concern to strategists as their company's own position. Understanding industry structure is also essential to effective strategic positioning. As we will see, defending against the competitive forces and shaping them in a company's favor are crucial to strategy.

Forces That Shape Competition. The configuration of the five forces differs by industry. In the market for commercial aircraft, fierce rivalry between dominant producers Airbus and Boeing and the bargaining power of the airlines that place huge orders for aircraft are strong, while the threat of entry, the threat of substitutes, and the power of suppliers are more benign. In the movie theater industry, the proliferation of substitute forms of entertainment and the power of the movie producers and distributors who supply movies, the critical input, are important.

The strongest competitive force or forces determine the profitability of an industry and become the most important to strategy formulation. The most salient force, however, is not always obvious.

For example, even though rivalry is often fierce in commodity industries, it may not be the factor limiting profitability. Low returns in the photographic film industry, for instance, are the result of a superior substitute product as Kodak and Fuji, the world's leading producers

21

of photographic film, learned with the advent of digital photography. In such a situation, coping with the substitute product becomes the number one strategic priority. Industry structure grows out of a set of economic and technical characteristics that determine the strength of each competitive force. We will examine these drivers in the pages that follow, taking the perspective of an incumbent, or a company already present in the industry. The analysis can be readily extended to understand the challenges facing a potential entrant.

Threat of entry. New entrants to an industry bring new capacity and a desire to gain market share that puts pressure on prices, costs, and the rate of investment necessary to compete. Particularly when new entrants are diversifying from other markets, they can leverage existing capabilities and cash flows to shake up competition, as Pepsi did when it entered the bottled water industry, Microsoft did when it began to offer internet browsers, and Apple did when it entered the music distribution business.

The threat of entry, therefore, puts a cap on the profit potential of an industry. When the threat is high, incumbents must hold down their prices or boost investment to deter new competitors. In specialty coffee retailing, for example, relatively low entry barriers mean that Starbucks must invest aggressively in modernizing stores and menus.

The threat of entry in an industry depends on the height of entry barriers that are present and on the reaction entrants can expect from incumbents. If entry barriers are low and newcomers expect little retaliation from the entrenched competitors, the threat of entry is high and industry profitability is moderated. It is the *threat* of entry, not whether entry actually occurs, that holds down profitability.

Barriers to entry. Entry barriers are advantages that incumbents have relative to new entrants.

There are seven major sources:

1. *Supply-side economies of scale.* These economies arise when firms that produce at larger volumes enjoy lower costs per unit because they can spread fixed costs over more units, employ more efficient technology, or command better terms from suppliers. Supplyside scale economies deter entry by forcing the aspiring entrant either to come into the industry on a large scale, which requires dislodging entrenched competitors, or to accept a cost disadvantage.

Scale economies can be found in virtually every activity in the value chain; which ones are most important varies by industry. In microprocessors, incumbents such as Intel are protected by scale economies in research, chip fabrication, and consumer marketing. For lawncare companies like Scotts Miracle-Gro, the most important scale economies are found in the supply chain and media advertising. In small-package delivery, economies of scale arise in national logistical systems and information technology.

2. *Demand-side benefits of scale.* These benefits, also known as network effects, arise in industries where a buyer's willingness to pay for a company's product increases with the number of other buyers who also patronize the company. Buyers may trust larger companies more for a crucial product: Recall the old adage that no one ever got fired for buying from IBM (when it was the dominant computer maker). Buyers may also value being in a "network" with a larger number of fellow customers. For instance, online auction participants are attracted to eBay because it offers the most potential trading partners. Demandside benefits of scale discourage entry by limiting the willingness of customers to buy from a newcomer and by reducing the price the newcomer can command until it builds up a large base of customers.

3. *Customer switching costs.* Switching costs are fixed costs that buyers face when they change suppliers. Such costs may arise because a buyer who switches vendors must, for example, alter product specifications, retrain employees to use a new product, or modify processes or information systems. The larger the switching costs, the harder it will be for an entrant to gain customers. Enterprise resource planning (ERP) software is an example of a product

with very high switching costs. Once a company has installed SAP's ERP system, for example, the costs of moving to a new vendor are astronomical because of embedded data, the fact that internal processes have been adapted to SAP, major retraining needs, and the mission-critical nature of the applications.

4. *Capital requirements.* The need to invest large financial resources in order to compete can deter new entrants. Capital may be necessary not only for fixed facilities but also to extend customer credit, build inventories, and fund start-up losses. The barrier is particularly great if the capital is required for unrecoverable and therefore harder-to-finance expenditures, such as up-front advertising or research and development. While major corporations have the financial resources to invade almost any industry, the huge capital requirements in certain fields limit the pool of likely entrants. Conversely, in such fields as tax preparation services or short-haul trucking, capital requirements are minimal and potential entrants plentiful.

It is important not to overstate the degree to which capital requirements alone deter entry. If industry returns are attractive and are expected to remain so, and if capital markets are efficient, investors will provide entrants with the funds they need. For aspiring air carriers, for instance, financing is available to purchase expensive aircraft because of their high resale value, one reason why there have been numerous new airlines in almost every region.

5. *Incumbency advantages independent of size.* No matter what their size, incumbents may have cost or quality advantages not available to potential rivals. These advantages can stem from such sources as proprietary technology, preferential access to the best raw material sources, preemption of the most favorable geographic locations, established brand identities, or cumulative experience that has allowed incumbents to learn how to produce more efficiently. Entrants try to bypass such advantages. Upstart discounters such as Target and Wal Mart, for example, have located stores in freestanding sites rather than regional shopping centers where established department stores were well entrenched.

6. *Unequal access to distribution channels.* The new entrant must, of course, secure distribution of its product or service. A new food item, for example, must displace others from the supermarket shelf via price breaks, promotions, intense selling efforts, or some other means. The more limited the wholesale or retail channels are and the more that existing competitors have tied them up, the tougher entry into an industry will be. Sometimes access to distribution is so high a barrier that new entrants must bypass distribution channels altogether or create their own. Thus, upstart low-cost airlines have avoided distribution through travel agents (who tend to favor established higher-fare carriers) and have encouraged passengers to book their own flights on the internet.

7. *Restrictive government policy.* Government policy can hinder or aid new entry directly, as well as amplify (or nullify) the other entry barriers. Government directly limits or even forecloses entry into industries through, for instance, licensing requirements and restrictions on foreign investment. Regulated industries like liquor retailing, taxi services, and airlines are visible examples. Government policy can heighten other entry barriers through such means as expansive patenting rules that protect proprietary technology from imitation or environmental or safety regulations that raise scale economies facing newcomers. Of course, government policies may also make entry easier directly through subsidies, for instance, or indirectly by funding basic research and making it available to all firms, new and old, reducing scale economies.Entry barriers should be assessed relative to the capabilities of potential entrants, which may be start-ups, foreign firms, or companies in related industries. And, as some of our examples illustrate, the strategist must be mindful of the creative ways newcomers might find to circumvent apparent barriers.

Expected retaliation. How potential entrants believe incumbents may react will also influence their decision to enter or stay out of an industry. If reaction is vigorous and protracted enough, the profit potential of participating in the industry can fall below the cost of capital.

Incumbents often use public statements and responses to one entrant to send a message to other prospective entrants about their commitment to defending market share.

Newcomers are likely to fear expected retaliation if: • Incumbents have previously responded vigorously to new entrants. • Incumbents possess substantial resources to fight back, including excess cash and unused borrowing power, available productive capacity, or clout with distribution channels and customers. • Incumbents seem likely to cut prices because they are committed to retaining market share at all costs or because the industry has high fixed costs, which create a strong motivation to drop prices to fill excess capacity. • Industry growth is slow so newcomers can gain volume only by taking it from incumbents. An analysis of barriers to entry and expected retaliation is obviously crucial for any company contemplating entry into a new industry. The challenge is to find ways to surmount the entry barriers without nullifying, through heavy investment, the profitability of participating in the industry:

The Five Forces That Shape Industry Competition

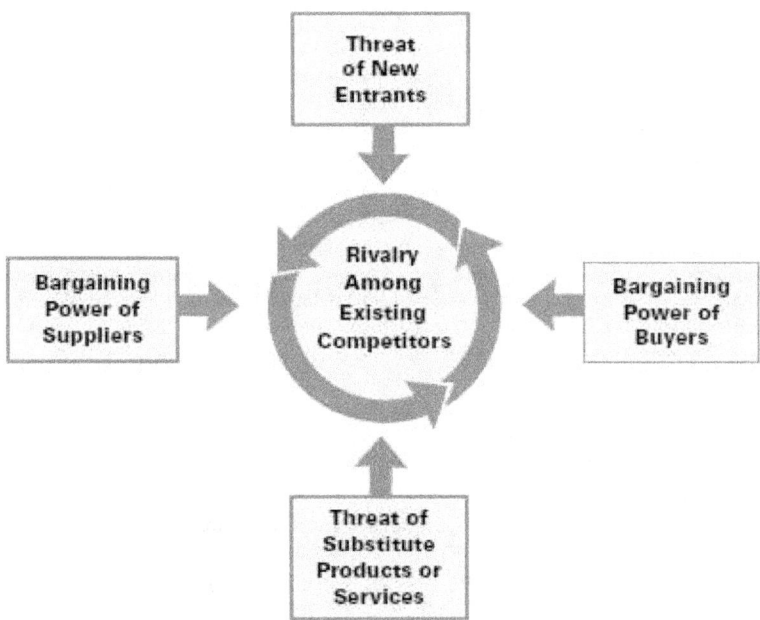

The power of suppliers. Powerful suppliers capture more of the value for themselves by charging higher prices, limiting quality or services, or shifting costs to industry participants. Powerful suppliers, including suppliers of labor, can squeeze profitability out of an industry that is unable to pass on cost increases in its own prices. Microsoft, for instance, has contributed to the erosion of profitability among personal computer makers by raising prices on operating systems. PC makers, competing fiercely for customers who can easily switch among them, have limited freedom to raise their prices accordingly.

Companies depend on a wide range of different supplier groups for inputs. A supplier group is powerful if:

- It is more concentrated than the industry it sells to. Microsoft's near monopoly in operating systems, coupled with the fragmentation of PC assemblers, exemplifies this situation.

- The supplier group does not depend heavily on the industry for its revenues. Suppliers serving many industries will not hesitate to extract maximum profits from each one. If a particular industry accounts for a large portion of a supplier group's volume or profit, however, suppliers will want to protect the industry through reasonable pricing and assist in activities such as R&D and lobbying.

- Industry participants face switching costs in changing suppliers. For example, shifting suppliers is difficult if companies have invested heavily in specialized ancillary equipment or in learning how to operate a supplier's equipment (as with Bloomberg terminals used by financial professionals). Or firms may have located their production lines adjacent to a supplier's manufacturing facilities (as in the case of some beverage companies and container manufacturers). When switching costs are high, industry participants find it hard to play suppliers off against one another. (Note that suppliers may have switching costs as well. This limits their power.)

- Suppliers offer products that are differentiated. Pharmaceutical companies that offer patented drugs with distinctive medical benefits have more power over hospitals, health maintenance organizations, and other drug buyers, for example, than drug companies offering me-too or generic products. There is no substitute for what the supplier group provides. Pilots' unions, for example, exercise considerable supplier power over airlines partly because there is no good alternative to a well-trained pilot in the cockpit. The supplier group can credibly threaten to integrate forward into the industry. In that case, if industry participants make too much money relative to suppliers, they will induce suppliers to enter the market.

The power of buyers. Powerful customers—the flip side of powerful suppliers—can capture more value by forcing down prices, demanding better quality or more service (thereby driving up costs), and generally playing industry participants off against one another, all at the expense of industry profitability. Buyers are powerful if they have negotiating leverage relative to industry participants, especially if they are price sensitive, using their clout primarily to pressure price reductions.

As with suppliers, there may be distinct groups of customers who differ in bargaining power. A customer group has negotiating leverage if:

- There are few buyers, or each one purchases in volumes that are large relative to the size of a single vendor. Large-volume buyers are particularly powerful in industries with high fixed costs, such as telecommunications equipment, offshore drilling, and bulk chemicals. High fixed costs and low marginal costs amplify the pressure on rivals to keep capacity filled through discounting.

- The industry's products are standardized or undifferentiated. If buyers believe they can always find an equivalent product, they tend to play one vendor against another.

- Buyers face few switching costs in changing vendors.

- Buyers can credibly threaten to integrate backward and produce the industry's product themselves if vendors are too profitable. Producers of soft drinks and beer have long controlled the power of packaging manufacturers by threatening to make, and at times actually making, packaging materials themselves. A buyer group is price sensitive if:

- The product it purchases from the industry represents a significant fraction of its cost structure or procurement budget. Here buyers are likely to shop around and bargain hard, as consumers do for home mortgages. Where the product sold by an industry is a small fraction of buyers' costs or expenditures, buyers are usually less price sensitive.

- The buyer group earns low profits, is strapped for cash, or is otherwise under pressure to trim its purchasing costs. Highly profitable or cash-rich customers, in contrast, are generally less price sensitive (that is, of course, if the item does not represent a large fraction of their costs).

- The quality of buyers' products or services is little affected by the industry's product. Where quality is very much affected by the industry's product, buyers are generally less price sensitive. When purchasing or renting production quality cameras, for instance, makers of major motion pictures opt for highly reliable equipment with the latest features. They pay limited attention to price.

- The industry's product has little effect on the buyer's other costs. Here, buyers focus on price. Conversely, where an industry's product or service can pay for itself many times over by improving performance or reducing labor, material, or other costs, buyers are usually more interested in quality than in price. Examples include products and services like tax accounting or well logging (which measures below-ground conditions of oil wells) that can save or even make the buyer money. Similarly, buyers tend not to be price sensitive in services such as investment banking, where poor performance can be costly and embarrassing.

Differences in Industry Profitability

The average return on invested capital varies markedly from industry to industry. Between 1992 and 2006, for example, average return on invested capital in U.S. industries ranged as low as zero or even negative to more than 50%. At the high end are industries like soft drinks and prepackaged software, which have been almost six times more profitable than the airline industry over the period.

Most sources of buyer power apply equally to consumers and to business-to-business customers. Like industrial customers, consumers tend to be more price sensitive if they are purchasing products that are undifferentiated, expensive relative to their incomes, and of a sort where product performance has limited consequences. The major difference with consumers is that their needs can be more intangible and harder to quantify.

Intermediate customers, or customers who purchase the product but are not the end user (such as assemblers or distribution channels), can be analyzed the same way as other buyers, with one important addition. Intermediate customers gain significant bargaining power when they can influence the purchasing decisions of customers downstream. Consumer electronics retailers, jewelry retailers, and agricultural equipment distributors are examples of distribution channels that exert a strong influence on end customers.

Producers often attempt to diminish channel clout through exclusive arrangements with particular distributors or retailers or by marketing directly to end users. Component manufacturers seek to develop power over assemblers by creating preferences for their components with downstream customers. Such is the case with bicycle parts and with sweeteners. DuPont has created enormous clout by advertising its Stainmaster brand of carpet fibers not only to the carpet manufacturers that actually buy them but also to downstream consumers. Many consumers request Stainmaster carpet even though DuPont is not a carpet manufacturer.

The threat of substitutes. A substitute performs the same or a similar function as an industry's product by a different means. Videoconferencing is a substitute for travel. Plastic is a substitute for aluminum. E-mail is a substitute for express mail. Sometimes, the threat of substitution is downstream or indirect, when a substitute replaces a buyer industry's product. For example, lawn-care products and services are threatened when multifamily homes in urban areas substitute for single-family homes in the suburbs. Software sold to agents is threatened when airline and travel websites substitute for travel agents.

Substitutes are always present, but they are easy to overlook because they may appear to be very different from the industry's product: To someone searching for a Father's Day gift, neckties and power tools may be substitutes. It is a substitute to do without, to purchase a used product rather than a new one, or to do it yourself (bring the service or product inhouse).

When the threat of substitutes is high, industry profitability suffers. Substitute products or services limit an industry's profit potential by placing a ceiling on prices. If an industry does not distance itself from substitutes through product performance, marketing, or other means, it will suffer in terms of profitability and often growth potential.

Substitutes not only limit profits in normal times, they also reduce the bonanza an industry can reap in good times. In emerging economies, for example, the surge in demand for wired telephone lines has been capped as many consumers opt to make a mobile telephone their first and only phone line.

The threat of a substitute is high if:

- It offers an attractive price-performance trade-off to the industry's product. The better the relative value of the substitute, the tighter is the lid on an industry's profit potential. For example, conventional providers of long-distance telephone service have suffered from the advent of inexpensive internet-based phone services such as Vonage and Skype. Similarly, video rental outlets are struggling with the emergence of cable and satellite video-on-demand services, online video rental services such as Netflix, and the rise of internet video sites like Google's YouTube.

- The buyer's cost of switching to the substitute is low. Switching from a proprietary, branded drug to a generic drug usually involves minimal costs, for example, which is why the shift to generics (and the fall in prices) is so substantial and rapid.

Strategists should be particularly alert to changes in other industries that may make them attractive substitutes when they were not before. Improvements in plastic materials, for example, allowed them to substitute for steel in many automobile components. In this way, technological changes or competitive discontinuities in seemingly unrelated businesses can have major impacts on industry profitability. Of course the substitution threat can also shift in favor of an industry, which bodes well for ist future profitability and growth potential.

Rivalry among existing competitors. Rivalry among existing competitors takes many familiar forms, including price discounting, new product introductions, advertising campaigns, and service improvements. High rivalry limits the profitability of an industry. The degree to which rivalry drives down an industry's profit potential depends, first, on the *intensity* with which companies compete and, second, on the *basis* on which they compete.

The intensity of rivalry is greatest if:

- Competitors are numerous or are roughly equal in size and power. In such situations, rivals find it hard to avoid poaching business. Without an industry leader, practices desirable for the industry as a whole go unenforced.

- Industry growth is slow. Slow growth precipitates fights for market share.

- Exit barriers are high. Exit barriers, the flip side of entry barriers, arise because of such things as highly specialized assets or management's devotion to a particular business. These barriers keep companies in the market even though they may be earning low or negative returns. Excess capacity remains in use, and the profitability of healthy competitors suffers as the sick ones hang on.

- Rivals are highly committed to the business and have aspirations for leadership, especially if they have goals that go beyond economic performance in the particular industry. High commitment to a business arises for a variety of reasons. For example, state-owned competitors may have goals that include employment or prestige. Units of larger companies may participate in an industry for image reasons or to offer a full line. Clashes of personality and ego have sometimes exaggerated rivalry to the detriment of profitability in fields such as the media and high technology.

- Firms cannot read each other's signals well because of lack of familiarity with one another, diverse approaches to competing, or differing goals.

The strength of rivalry reflects not just the intensity of competition but also the basis of competition. The *dimensions* on which competition takes place, and whether rivals converge to compete on the *same dimensions* , have a major influence on profitability.

Rivalry is especially destructive to profitability if it gravitates solely to price because price competition transfers profits directly from an industry to its customers. Price cuts are usually easy for competitors to see and match, making successive rounds of retaliation likely. Sustained price competition also trains customers to pay less attention to product features and service.

Price competition is most liable to occur if:

- Products or services of rivals are nearly identical and there are few switching costs for buyers. This encourages competitors to cut prices to win new customers. Years of airline price wars reflect these circumstances in that industry.

- Fixed costs are high and marginal costs are low. This creates intense pressure for competitors to cut prices below their average costs, even close to their marginal costs, to steal incremental customers while still making some contribution to covering fixed costs. Many basicmaterials businesses, such as paper and aluminum, suffer from this problem, especially if demand is not growing. So do delivery companies with fixed networks of routes that must be served regardless of volume.

- Capacity must be expanded in large increments to be efficient. The need for large capacity expansions, as in the polyvinyl chloride business, disrupts the industry's supply-demand balance and often leads to long and recurring periods of overcapacity and price cutting.

- The product is perishable. Perishability creates a strong temptation to cut prices and sell a product while it still has value. More products and services are perishable than is commonly thought. Just as tomatoes are perishable because they rot, models of computers are perishable because they soon become obsolete, and information may be perishable if it diffuses rapidly or becomes outdated, thereby losing ist value. Services such as hotel accommodations are perishable in the sense that unused capacity can never be recovered.

Competition on dimensions other than price on product features, support services, delivery time, or brand image, for instance—is less likely to erode profitability because it improves customer value and can support higher prices. Also, rivalry focused on such dimensions can improve value relative to substitutes or raise the barriers facing new entrants. While nonprice rivalry sometimes escalates to levels that undermine industry profitability, this is less likely to occur than it is with price rivalry.

As important as the dimensions of rivalry is whether rivals compete on the *same* dimensions.

When all or many competitors aim to meet the same needs or compete on the same attributes, the result is zero-sum competition. Here, one firm's gain is often another's loss, driving down profitability. While price competition runs a stronger risk than nonprice competition of becoming zero sum, this may not happen if companies take care to segment their markets, targeting their low-price offerings to different customers.

Rivalry can be positive sum, or actually increase the average profitability of an industry, when each competitor aims to serve the needs of different customer segments, with different mixes of price, products, services, features, or brand identities. Such competition can not only support higher average profitability but also expand the industry, as the needs of more customer groups are better met. The opportunity for positive-sum competition will be greater in industries serving diverse customer groups. With a clear understanding of the structural underpinnings of rivalry, strategists can sometimes take steps to shift the nature of competition in a more positive direction.

Factors, Not Forces. Industry structure, as manifested in the strength of the five competitive forces, determines the industry's long-run profit potential because it determines how the economic value created by the industry is divided how much is retained by companies in the industry versus bargained away by customers and suppliers, limited by substitutes, or constrained by potential new entrants. By considering all five forces, a strategist keeps overall structure in mind instead of gravitating to any one element. In addition, the strategist's attention remains focused on structural conditions rather than on fleeting factors.

It is especially important to avoid the common pitfall of mistaking certain visible attributes of an industry for its underlying structure. Consider the following:

Industry growth rate. A common mistake is to assume that fast-growing industries are always attractive. Growth does tend to mute rivalry, because an expanding pie offers opportunities for all competitors. But fast growth can put suppliers in a powerful position, and high growth with low entry barriers will draw in entrants. Even without new entrants, a high growth rate will not guarantee profitability if customers are powerful or substitutes are attractive. Indeed, some fast-growth businesses, such as personal computers, have been among the least profitable industries in recent years. A narrow focus on growth is one of the major causes of bad strategy decisions.

Technology and innovation. Advanced technology or innovations are not by themselves enough to make an industry structurally attractive (or unattractive). Mundane, low-technology industries with price-insensitive buyers, high switching costs, or high entry barriers arising from scale economies are often far more profitable than sexy industries, such as software and internet technologies, that attract competitors.

Government. Government is not best understood as a sixth force because government involvement is neither inherently good nor bad for industry profitability. The best way to understand the influence of government on competition is to analyze how specific government policies affect the five competitive forces. For instance, patents raise barriers to entry, boosting industry profit potential. Conversely, government policies favoring unions may raise supplier power and diminish profit potential. Bankruptcy rules that allow failing companies to reorganize rather than exit can lead to excess capacity and intense rivalry. Government operates at multiple levels and through many different policies, each of which will affect structure in different ways.

Complementary products and services. Complements are products or services used together with an industry's product. Complements arise when the customer benefit of two products combined is greater than the sum of each product's value in isolation. Computer hardware and software, for instance, are valuable together and worthless when separated.

In recent years, strategy researchers have highlighted the role of complements, especially in high-technology industries where they are most obvious. By no means, however, do complements appear only there. The value of a car, for example, is greater when the driver also has access to gasoline stations, roadside assistance, and auto insurance.

Complements can be important when they affect the overall demand for an industry's product. However, like government policy, complements are not a sixth force determining industry profitability since the presence of strong complements is not necessarily bad (or good) for industry profitability. Complements affect profitability through the way they influence the five forces.

The strategist must trace the positive or negative influence of complements on all five forces to ascertain their impact on profitability. The presence of complements can raise or lower barriers to entry. In application software, for example, barriers to entry were lowered when producers of complementary operating system software, notably Microsoft, provided tool sets making it easier to write applications. Conversely, the need to attract producers of complements can raise barriers to entry, as it does in video game hardware.

The presence of complements can also affect the threat of substitutes. For instance, the need for appropriate fueling stations makes it difficult for cars using alternative fuels to substitute for conventional vehicles. But complements can also make substitution easier. For example, Apple's iTunes hastened the substitution from CDs to digital music.

Complements can factor into industry rivalry either positively (as when they raise switching costs) or negatively (as when they neutralize product differentiation). Similar analyses can be done for buyer and supplier power. Sometimes companies compete by altering conditions in complementary industries in their favor, such as when videocassette-recorder producer JVC persuaded movie studios to favor its standard in issuing prerecorded tapes even though rival Sony's standard was probably superior from a technical standpoint.

Identifying complements is part of the analyst's work. As with government policies or important technologies, the strategic significance of complements will be best understood through the lens of the five forces.

Changes in Industry Structure. So far, we have discussed the competitive forces at a single point in time. Industry structure proves to be relatively stable, and industry profitability differences are remarkably persistent over time in practice. However, industry structure is constantly undergoing modest adjustment and occasionally it can change abruptly.

The Five Competitive Forces That Shape Strategy

Shifts in structure may emanate from outside an industry or from within. They can boost the industry's profit potential or reduce it. They may be caused by changes in technology, changes in customer needs, or other events. The five competitive forces provide a framework for identifying the most important industry developments and for anticipating their impact on industry attractiveness.

Shifting threat of new entry. Changes to any of the seven barriers described above can raise or lower the threat of new entry. The expiration of a patent, for instance, may unleash new entrants. On the day that Merck's patents for the cholesterol reducer Zocor expired, three pharmaceutical makers entered the market for the drug. Conversely, the proliferation of products in the ice cream industry has gradually filled up the limited freezer space in grocerystores, making it harder for new ice cream makers to gain access to distribution in North America and Europe.

Strategic decisions of leading competitors often have a major impact on the threat of entry. Starting in the 1970s, for example, retailers such as Wal-Mart, Kmart, and Toys "R" Us began to adopt new procurement, distribution, and inventory control technologies with large fixed costs, including automated distribution centers, bar coding, and point-of-sale terminals. These investments increased the economies of scale and made it more difficult for small retailers to enter the business (and for existing small players to survive).

Changing supplier or buyer power. As the factors underlying the power of suppliers and buyers change with time, their clout rises or declines. In the global appliance industry, for instance, competitors including Electrolux, General Electric, and Whirlpool have been squeezed by the consolidation of retail channels (the decline of appliance specialty stores, for instance, and the rise of big-box retailers like Best Buy and Home Depot in the United States). Another example is travel agents, who depend on airlines as a key supplier. When the internet allowed airlines to sell tickets directly to customers, this significantly increased their power to bargain down agents' commissions.

Shifting threat of substitution. The most common reason substitutes become more or less threatening over time is that advances in technology create new substitutes or shift price performance comparisons in one direction or the other. The earliest microwave ovens, for example, were large and priced above $2,000, making them poor substitutes for conventional ovens. With technological advances, they became serious substitutes. Flash computer memory has improved enough recently to become a meaningful substitute for low-capacity hard-disk drives. Trends in the availability or performance of complementary producers also shift the threat of substitutes.

New bases of rivalry. Rivalry often intensifies naturally over time. As an industry matures, growth slows. Competitors become more alike as industry conventions emerge, technology diffuses, and consumer tastes converge. Industry profitability falls, and weaker competitors are driven from the business. This story has played out in industry after industry; televisions, snowmobiles, and telecommunications equipment are just a few examples.

A trend toward intensifying price competition and other forms of rivalry, however, is by no means inevitable. For example, there has been enormous competitive activity in the U.S. casino industry in recent decades, but most of it has been positive-sum competition directed toward new niches and geographic segments (such as riverboats, trophy properties, Native American reservations, international expansion, and novel customer groups like families). Head-to-head rivalry that lowers prices or boosts the payouts to winners has been limited.

The nature of rivalry in an industry is altered by mergers and acquisitions that introduce new capabilities and ways of competing. Or, technological innovation can reshape rivalry. In the retail brokerage industry, the advent of the internet lowered marginal costs and reduced differentiation, triggering far more intense competition on commissions and fees than in the past.

The Five Competitive Forces That Shape Strategy

In some industries, companies turn to mergers and consolidation not to improve cost and quality but to attempt to stop intense competition. Eliminating rivals is a risky strategy, however. The five competitive forces tell us that a profit windfall from removing today's competitors often attracts new competitors and backlash from customers and suppliers. In New York banking, for example, the 1980s and 1990s saw escalating consolidations of commercial and savings banks, including Manufacturers Hanover, Chemical, Chase, and Dime Savings. But today the retail-banking landscape of Manhattan is as diverse as ever, as new entrants such as Wachovia, Bank of America, and Washington Mutual have entered the market.

Implications for Strategy. Understanding the forces that shape industry competition is the starting point for developing strategy. Every company should already know what the average profitability of its industry is and how that has been changing over time. The five forces reveal *why* industry profitability is what it is. Only then can a company incorporate industry conditions into strategy.

The forces reveal the most significant aspects of the competitive environment. They also provide a baseline for sizing up a company's strengths and weaknesses: Where does the company stand versus buyers, suppliers, entrants, rivals, and substitutes? Most importantly, an understanding of industry structure guides managers toward fruitful possibilities for strategic action, which may include any or all of the following: positioning the company to better cope with the current competitive forces; anticipating and exploiting shifts in the forces; and shaping the balance of forces to create a new industry structure that is more favorable to the company. The best strategies exploit more than one of these possibilities.

Positioning the company. Strategy can be viewed as building defenses against the competitive forces or finding a position in the industry where the forces are weakest. Consider, for instance, the position of Paccar in the market for heavy trucks. The heavy-truck industry is structurally challenging. Many buyers operate large fleets or are large leasing companies, with both the leverage and the motivation to drive down the price of one of their largest purchases. Most trucks are built to regulated standards and offer similar features, so price competition is rampant. Capital intensity causes rivalry to be fierce, especially during the recurring cyclical downturns. Unions exercise considerable supplier power. Though there are few direct substitutes for an 18-wheeler, truck buyers face important substitutes for their services, such as cargo delivery by rail.

In this setting, Paccar, a Bellevue, Washington based company with about 20% of the North American heavy-truck market, has cho sen to focus on one group of customers: owneroperators drivers who own their trucks and contract directly with shippers or serve as subcontractors to larger trucking companies. Such small operators have limited clout as truck buyers. They are also less price sensitive because of their strong emotional ties to and economic dependence on the product. They take great pride in their trucks, in which they spend most of their time.

Paccar has invested heavily to develop an array of features with owner-operators in mind: luxurious sleeper cabins, plush leather seats, noise-insulated cabins, sleek exterior styling, and so on. At the company's extensive network of dealers, prospective buyers use software to select among thousands of options to put their personal signature on their trucks. These customized trucks are built to order, not to stock, and delivered in six to eight weeks. Paccar's trucks also have aerodynamic designs that reduce fuel consumption, and they maintain their resale value better than other trucks. Paccar's roadside assistance program and ITsupported system for distributing spare parts reduce the time a truck is out of service. All these are crucial considerations for an owneroperator. Customers pay Paccar a 10% premium, and its Kenworth and Peterbilt brands are considered status symbols at truck stops.

32

The Five Competitive Forces That Shape Strategy

Paccar illustrates the principles of positioning a company within a given industry structure. The firm has found a portion of its industry where the competitive forces are weaker where it can avoid buyer power and pricebased rivalry. And it has tailored every single part of the value chain to cope well with the forces in its segment. As a result, Paccar has been profitable for 68 years straight and has earned a long-run return on equity above 20%.

In addition to revealing positioning opportunities within an existing industry, the five forces framework allows companies to rigorously analyze entry and exit. Both depend on answering the difficult question: "What is the potential of this business?" Exit is indicated when industry structure is poor or declining and the company has no prospect of a superior positioning. In considering entry into a new industry, creative strategists can use the framework to spot an industry with a good future before this good future is reflected in the prices of acquisition candidates. Five forces analysis may also reveal industries that are not necessarily attractive for the average entrant but in which a company has good reason to believe it can surmount entry barriers at lower cost than most firms or has a unique ability to cope with the industry's competitive forces.

Exploiting industry change. Industry changes bring the opportunity to spot and claim promising new strategic positions if the strategist has a sophisticated understanding of the competitive forces and their underpinnings. Consider, for instance, the evolution of the music industry during the past decade. With the advent of the internet and the digital distribution of music, some analysts predicted the birth of thousands of music labels (that is, record companies that develop artists and bring their music to market). This, the analystsargued, would break a pattern that had held since Edison invented the phonograph: Between three and six major record companies had always dominated the industry. The internet would, they predicted, remove distribution as a barrier to entry, unleashing a flood of new players into the music industry.

A careful analysis, however, would have revealed that physical distribution was not the crucial barrier to entry. Rather, entry was barred by other benefits that large music labels enjoyed. Large labels could pool the risks of developing new artists over many bets, cushioning the impact of inevitable failures. Even more important, they had advantages in breaking through the clutter and getting their new artists heard. To do so, they could promise radio stations and record stores access to wellknown artists in exchange for promotion of new artists. New labels would find this nearly impossible to match. The major labels stayed the course, and new music labels have been rare.

This is not to say that the music industry is structurally unchanged by digital distribution. Unauthorized downloading created an illegal but potent substitute. The labels tried for years to develop technical platforms for digital distribution themselves, but major companies hesitated to sell their music through a platform owned by a rival. Into this vacuum stepped Apple with its iTunes music store, launched in 2003 to support its iPod music player. By permitting the creation of a powerful new gatekeeper, the major labels allowed industry structure to shift against them. The number of major record companies has actually de clined—from six in 1997 to four today as companies struggled to cope with the digital phenomenon.

When industry structure is in flux, new and promising competitive positions may appear. Structural changes open up new needs and new ways to serve existing needs. Established leaders may overlook these or be constrained by past strategies from pursuing them. Smaller competitors in the industry can capitalize on such changes, or the void may well be filled by new entrants.

Shaping industry structure. When a company exploits structural change, it is recognizing, and reacting to, the inevitable. However, companies also have the ability to shape industry structure. A firm can lead its industry toward new ways of competing that alter the five forces for the better. In reshaping structure, a company wants its competitors to follow so that the entire industry will be transformed. While many industry participants may benefit in the process, the innovator can benefit most if it can shift competition in directions where it can excel.

An industry's structure can be reshaped in two ways: by redividing profitability in favor of incumbents or by expanding the overall profit pool. Redividing the industry pie aims to increase the share of profits to industry competitors instead of to suppliers, buyers, substitutes, and keeping out potential entrants. Expanding the profit pool involves increasing the overall pool of economic value generated by the industry in which rivals, buyers, and suppliers can all share.

Redividing profitability. To capture more profits for industry rivals, the starting point is to determine which force or forces are currently constraining industry profitability and address them. A company can potentially influence all of the competitive forces. The strategist's goal here is to reduce the share of profits that leak to suppliers, buyers, and substitutes or are sacrificed to deter entrants.

To neutralize supplier power, for example, a firm can standardize specifications for parts to make it easier to switch among suppliers. It can cultivate additional vendors, or alter technology to avoid a powerful supplier group altogether. To counter customer power, companies may expand services that raise buyers' switching costs or find alternative means of reaching customers to neutralize powerful channels. To temper profit-eroding price rivalry, companies can invest more heavily in unique products, as pharmaceutical firms have done, or expand support services to customers. To scare off entrants, incumbents can elevate the fixed cost of competing—for instance, by escalating their R&D or marketing expenditures. To limit the threat of substitutes, companies can offer better value through new features or wider product accessibility. When soft-drink producers introduced vending machines and convenience store channels, for example, they dramatically improved the availability of soft drinks relative to other beverages.

Sysco, the largest food-service distributor in North America, offers a revealing example of how an industry leader can change the structure of an industry for the better. Food-service distributors purchase food and related items from farmers and food processors. They then warehouse and deliver these items to restaurants, hospitals, employer cafeterias, schools, and other food-service institutions. Given low barriers to entry, the food-service distribution industry has historically been highly fragmented, with numerous local competitors. While rivals try to cultivate customer relationships, buyers are price sensitive because food represents a large share of their costs. Buyers can also choose the substitute approaches of purchasing directly from manufacturers or using retail sources, avoiding distributors altogether. Suppliers wield bargaining power: They are often large companies with strong brand names that food preparers and consumers recognize. Average profitability in the industry has been modest.

Sysco recognized that, given its size and national reach, it might change this state of affairs. It led the move to introduce private-label distributor brands with specifications tailored to the food-service market, moderating supplier power. Sysco emphasized value-added services to buyers such as credit, menu planning, and inventory management to shift the basis of competition away from just price. These moves, together with stepped-up investments in information technology and regional distribution centers, substantially raised the bar for new entrants while making the substitutes less attractive. Not surprisingly, the industry has been consolidating, and industry profitability appears to be rising.

Industry leaders have a special responsibility for improving industry structure. Doing so often requires resources that only large players possess. Moreover, an improved industry structure is a public good because it benefits every firm in the industry, not just the company that initiated the improvement. Often, it is more in the interests of an industry leader than any other participant to invest for the common good because leaders will usually benefit the most. Indeed, improving the industry may be a leader's most profitable strategic opportunity, in part because attempts to gain further market share can trigger strong reactions from rivals, customers, and even suppliers.

There is a dark side to shaping industry structure that is equally important to understand. Ill-advised changes in competitive positioning and operating practices can *undermine* industry structure. Faced with pressures to gain market share or enamored with innovation for its own sake, managers may trigger new kinds of competition that no incumbent can win. When taking actions to improve their own company's competitive advantage, then, strategists should ask whether they are setting in motion dynamics that will undermine industry structure in the long run. In the early days of the personal computer industry, for instance, IBM tried to make up for its late entry by offering an open architecture that would set industry standards and attract complementary makers of application software and peripherals. In the process, it ceded ownership of the critical components of the PC—the operating system and the microprocessor—to Microsoft and Intel. By standardizing PCs, it encouraged price-based rivalry and shifted power to suppliers. Consequently, IBM became the temporarily dominant firm in an industry with an enduringly unattractive structure.

Expanding the profit pool. When overall demand grows, the industry's quality level rises, intrinsic costs are reduced, or waste is eliminated, the pie expands. The total pool of value available to competitors, suppliers, and buyers grows. The total profit pool expands, for example, when channels become more competitive or when an industry discovers latent buyers for its product that are not currently being served. When soft-drink producers rationalized their independent bottler networks to make them more efficient and effective, both the soft-drink companies and the bottlers benefited. Overall value can also expand when firms work collaboratively with suppliers to improve coordination and limit unnecessary costs incurred in the supply chain. This lowers the inherent cost structure of the industry, allowing higher profit, greater demand through lower prices, or both. Or, agreeing on quality standards can bring up industrywide quality and service levels, and hence prices, benefiting rivals, suppliers, and customers.

Expanding the overall profit pool creates win-win opportunities for multiple industry participants. It can also reduce the risk of destructive rivalry that arises when incumbents attempt to shift bargaining power or capture more market share. However, expanding the pie does not reduce the importance of industry structure. How the expanded pie is divided will ultimately be determined by the five forces. The most successful companies are those that expand the industry profit pool in ways that allow them to share disproportionately in the benefits.

Defining the industry. The five competitive forces also hold the key to defining the relevant industry (or industries) in which a company competes. Drawing industry boundaries correctly, around the arena in which competition actually takes place, will clarify the causes of profitability and the appropriate unit for setting strategy. A company needs a separate strategy for each distinct industry. Mistakes in industry definition made by competitors present opportunities for staking out superior strategic positions. (See the sidebar "Defining the Relevant Industry.")

Competition and Value. The competitive forces reveal the drivers of industry competition. A company strategist who understands that competition extends well beyond existing rivals will detect wider competitive threats and be better equipped to address them. At the same time, thinking comprehensively about an industry's structure can uncover opportunities: differences in customers, suppliers, substitutes, potential entrants, and rivals that can become the basis for distinct strategies yielding superior performance. In a world of more open competition and relentless change, it is more important than ever to think structurally about competition.

The Five Competitive Forces That Shape Strategy

Understanding industry structure is equally important for investors as for managers. The five competitive forces reveal whether an industry is truly attractive, and they help investors anticipate positive or negative shifts in industry structure before they are obvious. The five forces distinguish short-term blips from structural changes and allow investors to take advantage of undue pessimism or optimism. Those companies whose strategies have industry- transforming potential become far clearer. This deeper thinking about competition is a more powerful way to achieve genuine investment success than the financial projections and trend extrapolation that dominate today's investment analysis.

If both executives and investors looked at competition this way, capital markets would be a far more effective force for company success and economic prosperity. Executives and investors would both be focused on the same fundamentals that drive sustained profitability. The conversation between investors and executives would focus on the structural, not the transient. Imagine the improvement in company performance and in the economy as a whole—if all the energy expended in "pleasing the Street" were redirected toward the factors that create true economic value.

Common Pitfalls In conducting the analysis avoid the following common mistakes:

- Defining the industry too broadly or too narrowly. • Making lists instead of engaging in rigorous analysis.

- Paying equal attention to all of the forces rather than digging deeply into the most important ones.

- Confusing effect (price sensitivity) with cause (buyer economics).Using static analysis that ignores industry trends.

- Confusing cyclical or transient changes with true structural changes.

- Using the framework to declare an industry attractive or unattractive rather than using it to guide strategic choices.

Typical Steps in Industry Analysis

Define the relevant industry:

- What products are in it? Which ones are part of another distinct industry?

- What is the geographic scope of competition?

Identify the participants and segment them into groups, if appropriate:

Who are

- the buyers and buyer groups?

- the suppliers and supplier groups?

- the competitors?

- the substitutes?

- the potential entrants?

Assess the underlying drivers of each competitive force to determine which forces are strong and which are weak and why.

Determine overall industry structure, and test the analysis for consistency:

- Why is the level of profitability what it is?

- Which are the controlling forces for profitability?

- Is the industry analysis consistent with actual long-run profitability?

- Are more-profitable players better positioned in relation to the five forces?

The Five Competitive Forces That Shape Strategy

Analyze recent and likely future changes in each force, both positive and negative.

Identify aspects of industry structure that might be influenced by competitors, by new entrants, or by your company.

Defining the Relevant Industry. Defining the industry in which competition actually takes place is important for good industry analysis, not to mention for developing strategy and setting business unit boundaries. Many strategy errors emanate from mistaking the relevant industry, defining it too broadly or too narrowly. Defining the industry too broadly obscures differences among products, customers, or geographic regions that are important to competition, strategic positioning, and profitability. Defining the industry too narrowly overlooks commonalities and linkages across related products or geographic markets that are crucial to competitive advantage. Also, strategists must be sensitive to the possibility that industry boundaries can shift.

The boundaries of an industry consist of two primary dimensions. First is the *scope of products or services.*. For example, is motor oil used in cars part of the same industry as motor oil used in heavy trucks and stationary engines, or are these different industries? The second dimension is *geographic scope* . Most industries are present in many parts of the world. However, is competition contained within each state, or is it national? Does competition take place within regions such as Europe or North America, or is there a single global industry?

The five forces are the basic tool to resolve these questions. If industry structure for two products is the same or very similar (that is, if they have the same buyers, suppliers, barriers to entry, and so forth), then the products are best treated as being part of the same industry. If industry structure differs markedly, however, the two products may be best understood as separate industries.

In lubricants, the oil used in cars is similar or even identical to the oil used in trucks, but the similarity largely ends there. Automotive motor oil is sold to fragmented, generally unsophisticated customers through numerous and often powerful channels, using extensive advertising. Products are packaged in small containers and logistical costs are high, necessitating local production. Truck and power generation lubricants are sold to entirely different buyers in entirely different ways using a separate supply chain. Industry structure (buyer power, barriers to entry, and so forth) is substantially different. Automotive oil is thus a distinct industry from oil for truck and stationary engine uses. Industry profitability will differ in these two cases, and a lubricant company will need a separate strategy for competing in each area.

Differences in the five competitive forces also reveal the geographic scope of competition. If an industry has a similar structure in every country (rivals, buyers, and so on), the presumption is that competition is global, and the five forces analyzed from a global perspective will set average profitability. A single global strategy is needed. If an industry has quite different structures in different geographic regions, however, each region may well be a distinct industry. Otherwise, competition would have leveled the differences. The five forces analyzed for each region will set profitability there.

The extent of differences in the five forces for related products or across geographic areas is a matter of degree, making industry definition often a matter of judgment. A rule of thumb is that where the differences in any one force are large, and where the differences involve more than one force, distinct industries may well be present.

Fortunately, however, even if industry boundaries are drawn incorrectly, careful five forces analysis should reveal important competitive threats. A closely related product omitted from the industry definition will show up as a substitute, for example, or competitors overlooked as rivals will be recognized as potential entrants. At the same time, the five forces analysis should reveal major differences within overly broad industries that will indicate the need to adjust industry boundaries or strategies.

Industry Analysis in Practice Good industry analysis looks rigorously at the structural underpinnings of profitability. A first step is to understand the appropriate time horizon.

One of the essential tasks in industry analysis is to distinguish temporary or cyclical changes from structural changes. A good guideline for the appropriate time horizon is the full business cycle for the particular industry. For most industries, a three-to-five-year horizon is appropriate, although in some industries with long lead times, such as mining, the appropriate horizon might be a decade or more. It is average profitability over this period, not profitability in any particular year, that should be the focus of analysis.

The point of industry analysis is not to declare the industry attractive or unattractive but to understand the underpinnings of competition and the root causes of profitability.

As much as possible, analysts should look at industry structure quantitatively, rather than be satisfied with lists of qualitative factors. Many elements of the five forces can be quantified: the percentage of the buyer's total cost accounted for by the industry's product (to understand buyer price sensitivity); the percentage of industry sales required to fill a plant or operate a logistical network of efficient scale (to help assess barriers to entry); the buyer's switching cost (determining the inducement an entrant or rival must offer customers).

The strength of the competitive forces affects prices, costs, and the investment required to compete; thus the forces are directly tied to the income statements and balance sheets of industry participants.

Industry structure defines the gap between revenues and costs. For example, intense rivalry drives down prices or elevates the costs of marketing, R&D, or customer service, reducing margins. How much? Strong suppliers drive up input costs. How much? Buyer power lowers prices or elevates the costs of meeting buyers' demands, such as the requirement to hold more inventory or provide financing. How much? Low barriers to entry or close substitutes limit the level of sustainable prices. How much? It is these economic relationships that sharpen the strategist's understanding of industry competition.

Finally, good industry analysis does not just list pluses and minuses but sees an industry in overall, systemic terms.

Which forces are underpinning (or constraining) today's profitability? How might shifts in one competitive force trigger reactions in others? Answering such questions is often the source of true strategic insights.

The Idea in Brief

You know that to sustain long-term profitability you must respond strategically to competition. And you naturally keep tabs on your established rivals. But as you scan the competitive arena, are you also looking *beyond* your direct competitors? As Porter explains in this update of his revolutionary 1979 HBR article, four additional competitive forces can hurt your prospective profits:

- Savvy customers can force down prices by playing you and your rivals against one another.

- Powerful suppliers may constrain your profits if they charge higher prices.

- Aspiring entrants , armed with new capacity and hungry for market share, can ratchet up the investment required for you to stay in the game.

- Substitute offerings can lure customers away.

Consider commercial aviation: It's one of the least profitable industries because all five forces are strong. Established rivals compete intensely on price. Customers are fickle, searching for the best deal regardless of carrier. Suppliers—plane and engine manufacturers, along with unionized labor forces—bargain away the lion's share of airlines' profits. New players enter the industry in a constant stream. And substitutes are readily available such as train or car travel.

By analyzing all five competitive forces, you gain a complete picture of what's influencing profitability in your industry. You identify game-changing trends early, so you can swiftly exploit them. And you spot ways to work around constraints on profitability or even reshape the forces in your favor.

By understanding how the five competitive forces influence profitability in your industry, you can develop a strategy for enhancing your company's long-term profits. Porter suggests the following:

POSITION YOUR COMPANY WHERE THE FORCES ARE WEAKEST

Example: In the heavy-truck industry, many buyers operate large fleets and are highly motivated to drive down truck prices. Trucks are built to regulated standards and offer similar features, so price competition is stiff; unions exercise considerable supplier power; and buyers can use substitutes such as cargo delivery by rail.

To create and sustain long-term profitability within this industry, heavy-truck maker Paccar chose to focus on one customer group where competitive forces are weakest: individual drivers who own their trucks and contract directly with suppliers. These operators have limited clout as buyers and are less price sensitive because of their emotional ties to and economic dependence on their own trucks.

For these customers, Paccar has developed such features as luxurious sleeper cabins, plush leather seats, and sleek exterior styling. Buyers can select from thousands of options to put their personal signature on these built-to-order trucks.

Customers pay Paccar a 10% premium, and the company has been profitable for 68 straight years and earned a long-run return on equity above 20%.

EXPLOIT CHANGES IN THE FORCES

Example: With the advent of the Internet and digital distribution of music, unauthorized downloading created an illegal but potent substitute for record companies' services. The record companies tried to develop technical platforms for digital distribution themselves, but major labels didn't want to sell their music through a platform owned by a rival.

Into this vacuum stepped Apple, with ist iTunes music store supporting its iPod music player. The birth of this powerful new gatekeeper has whittled down the number of major labels from six in 1997 to four today.

RESHAPE THE FORCES IN YOUR FAVOR

Use tactics designed specifically to reduce the share of profits leaking to other players. For example:

- To neutralize supplier power, standardize specifications for parts so your company can switch more easily among vendors.

- To counter customer power , expand your services so it's harder for customers to leave you for a rival.

- To temper price wars initiated by established rivals , invest more heavily in products that differ significantly from competitors' offerings.

- To scare off new entrants , elevate the fixed costs of competing; for instance, by escalating your R&D expenditures.

- To limit the threat of substitutes, offer better value through wider product accessibility. Soft-drink producers did this by introducing vending machines and convenience store channels, which dramatically improved the availability of soft drinks relative to other beverages.

CHAPTER 3

The Secrets to Successful Strategy Execution

Research shows that enterprises fail at execution because they go straight to structural reorganization and neglect the most powerful drivers of effectiveness—decision rights and information flow. by Gary L. Neilson, Karla L. Martin, and Elizabeth Powers

A brilliant strategy, blockbuster product, or breakthrough technology can put you on the competitive map, but only solid execution can keep you there. You have to be able to deliver on your intent. Unfortunately, the majority of companies aren't very good at it, by their own admission. Over the past five years, we have invited many thousands of employees (about 25% of whom came from executive ranks) to complete an online assessment of their organizations' capabilities, a process that's generated a database of 125,000 profiles representing more than 1,000 companies, government agencies, and not-for-profits in over 50 countries. Employees at three out of every five companies rated their organization weak at execution—that is, when asked if they agreed with the statement "Important strategic and operational decisions are quickly translated into action," the majority answered no.

Execution is the result of thousands of decisions made every day by employees acting according to the information they have and their own self-interest. In our work helping more than 250 companies learn to execute more effectively, we've identified four fundamental building blocks executives can use to influence those actions—clarifying decision rights, designing information flows, aligning motivators, and making changes to structure. (For simplicity's sake we refer to them as decision rights, information, motivators, and structure.)

In efforts to improve performance, most organizations go right to structural measures because moving lines around the org chart seems the most obvious solution and the changes are visible and concrete. Such steps generally reap some short-term efficiencies quickly, but in so doing address only the symptoms of dysfunction, not its root causes. Several years later, companies usually end up in the same place they started. Structural change can and should be part of the path to improved execution, but it's best to think of it as the capstone, not the cornerstone, of any organizational transformation. In fact, our research shows that actions having to do with decision rights and information are far more important—about twice as effective—as improvements made to the other two building blocks.

Take, for example, the case of a global consumer packaged-goods company that lurched down the reorganization path in the early 1990s. (We have altered identifying details in this and other cases that follow.) Disappointed with company performance, senior management did what most companies were doing at that time: They restructured. They eliminated some layers of management and broadened spans of control. Managementstaffing costs quickly fell by 18%. Eight years later, however, it was déjà vu. The layers had crept back in, and spans of control had once again narrowed. In addressing only structure, management had attacked the visible symptoms of poor performance but not the underlying cause—how people made decisions and how they were held accountable.

This time, management looked beyond lines and boxes to the mechanics of how work got done. Instead of searching for ways to strip out costs, they focused on improving execution and in the process discovered the true reasons for the performance shortfall. Managers didn't have a clear sense of their respective roles and responsibilities. They did not intuitively

41

understand which decisions were theirs to make. Moreover, the link between performance and rewards was weak. This was a company long on micromanaging and second-guessing, and short on accountability. Middle managers spent 40% of their time justifying and reporting upward or questioning the tactical decisions of their direct reports.

Armed with this understanding, the company designed a new management model that established who was accountable for what and made the connection between performance and reward. For instance, the norm at this company, not unusual in the industry, had been to promote people quickly, within 18 months to two years, before they had a chance to see their initiatives through. As a result, managers at every level kept doing their old jobs even after they had been promoted, peering over the shoulders of the direct reports who were now in charge of their projects and, all too frequently, taking over. Today, people stay in their positions longer so they can follow through on their own initiatives, and they're still around when the fruits of their labors start to kick in. What's more, results from those initiatives continue to count in their performance reviews for some time after they've been promoted, forcing managers to live with the expectations they'd set in their previous jobs. As a consequence, forecasting has become more accurate and reliable. These actions did yield a structure with fewer layers and greater spans of control, but that was a side effect, not the primary focus, of the changes.

The Elements of Strong Execution. Our conclusions arise out of decades of practical application and intensive research. Nearly five years ago, we and our colleagues set out to gather empirical data to identify the actions that were most effective in enabling an organization to implement strategy. What particular ways of restructuring, motivating, improving information flows, and clarifying decision rights mattered the most? We started by drawing up a list of 17 traits, each corresponding to one or more of the four building blocks we knew could enable effective execution traits like the free flow of information across organizational boundaries or the degree to which senior leaders refrain from getting involved in operating decisions. With these factors in mind, we developed an online profiler that allows individuals to assess the execution

capabilities of their organizations. Over the next four years or so, we collected data from many thousands of profiles, which in turn allowed us to more precisely calibrate the impact of each trait on an organization's ability to execute. That allowed us to rank all 17 traits in order of their relative influence.

Ranking the traits makes clear how important decision rights and information are to effective strategy execution. The first eight traits map directly to decision rights and information. Only three of the 17 traits relate to structure, and none of those ranks higher than 13th. We'll walk through the top five traits here.

1. Everyone has a good idea of the decisions and actions for which he or she is responsible. In companies strong on execution, 71% of individuals agree with this statement; that figure drops to 32% in organizations weak on execution.

Blurring of decision rights tends to occur as a company matures. Young organizations are generally too busy getting things done to define roles and responsibilities clearly at the outset. And why should they? In a small company, it's not so difficult to know what other people are up to. So for a time, things work out well enough. As the company grows, however, executives come and go, bringing in with them and taking away different expectations, and over time the approval process gets ever more convoluted and murky. It becomes increasingly unclear where one person's accountability begins and another's ends.

One global consumer-durables company found this out the hard way. It was so rife with people making competing and conflicting decisions that it was hard to find anyone below the CEO who felt truly accountable for profitability. The company was organized into 16 product divisions aggregated into three geographic groups—North America, Europe, and International. Each of the divisions was charged with reaching explicit performance targets, but functional staff at corporate headquarters controlled spending targets how R&D dollars were allocated, for instance. Decisions made by divisional and geographic leaders were routinely overridden by functional leaders. Overhead costs began to mount as the divisions added staff to help them create bulletproof cases to challenge corporate decisions.

Decisions stalled while divisions negotiated with functions, each layer weighing in with questions. Functional staffers in the divisions (financial analysts, for example) often deferred to their higher-ups in corporate rather than their division vice president, since functional leaders were responsible for rewards and promotions. Only the CEO and his executive team had the discretion to resolve disputes. All of these symptoms fed on one another and collectively hampered execution—until a new CEO came in.

The new chief executive chose to focus less on cost control and more on profitable growth by redefining the divisions to focus on consumers. As part of the new organizational model, the CEO designated accountability for profits unambiguously to the divisions and also gave them the authority to draw on functional activities to support their goals (as well as more control of the budget). Corporate functional roles and decision rights were recast to better support the divisions' needs and also to build the cross-divisional links necessary for developing the global capabilities of the business as a whole. For the most part, the functional leaders understood the market realities—and that change entailed some adjustments to the operating model of the business. It helped that the CEO brought them into the organizational redesign process, so that the new model wasn't something imposed on them as much as it was something they engaged in and built together.

2. Important information about the competitive environment gets to headquarters quickly. On average, 77% of individuals in strong-execution organizations agree with this statement, whereas only 45% of those in weak-execution organizations do. Headquarters can serve a powerful function in identifying patterns and promulgating best practices throughout business segments and geographic regions. But it can play this coordinating role only if it has accurate and up-to-date market intelligence. Otherwise, it will tend to impose its own agenda and policies rather than defer to operations that are much closer to the customer.

Consider the case of heavy-equipment manufacturer Caterpillar.

Today it is a highly successful $45 billion global company, but a generation ago, Caterpillar's organization was so badly misaligned that its very existence was threatened. Decision rights were hoarded at the top by functional general offices located at headquarters in Peoria, Illinois, while much of the information needed to make those decisions resided in the field with sales managers. "It just took a long time to get decisions going up and down the functional silos, and they really weren't good business decisions; they were more functional decisions," noted one field executive. Current CEO Jim Owens, then a managing director in Indonesia, told us that such information that did make it to the top had been "whitewashed and varnished several times over along the way." Cut off from information about the external market, senior executives focused on the organization's internal workings, overanalyzing issues and second-guessing decisions made at lower levels, costing the company opportunities in fast-moving markets. Pricing, for example, was based on cost and determined not by market realities but by the pricing general office in Peoria. Sales representatives across the world lost sale after sale to Komatsu, whose competitive pricing consistently beat Caterpillar's. In 1982, the company posted the first annual loss in its almost-60-year history. In 1983 and 1984, it lost $1 million a day, seven days a week. By the end of 1984, Caterpillar had lost a billion dollars. By 1988, then-CEO George Schaefer stood atop an entrenched bureaucracy that was, in his words, "telling me what I wanted to hear, not what I needed to know." So, he convened a task force of "renegade" middle managers and tasked them with charting Caterpillar's future.

Ironically, the way to ensure that the right information flowed to headquarters was to make sure the right decisions were made much further down the organization. By delegating operational responsibility to the people closer to the action, top executives were free to focus on more global strategic issues. Accordingly, the company reorganized into business units, making each accountable for its own P&L statement. The functional general offices that had been all-powerful ceased to exist, literally overnight. Their talent and expertise, including engineering, pricing, and manufacturing, were parceled out to the new business units, which could now design their own products, develop their own manufacturing processes and schedules, and set their own prices. The move dramatically decentralized decision rights, giving the units control over market decisions. The business unit P&Ls were now measured consistently across the enterprise, as return on assets became the universal measure of success. With this accurate, up-to-date, and directly comparable information, senior decision makers at headquarterscould make smart strategic choices and tradeoffs rather than use outdated sales data to make ineffective, tactical marketing decisions.

Within 18 months, the company was working in the new model. "This was a revolution that became a renaissance," Owens recalls, "a spectacular transformation of a kind of sluggish company into one that actually has entrepreneurial zeal. And that transition was very quick because it was decisive and it was complete; it was thorough; it was universal, worldwide, all at one time.

3. Once made, decisions are rarely second-guessed. Whether someone is secondguessing depends on your vantage point. A more senior and broader enterprise perspective can add value to a decision, but managers up the line may not be adding incremental value; instead, they may be stalling progress by redoing their subordinates' jobs while, in effect, shirking their own. In our research, 71% of respondents in weak-execution companies thought that decisions were being secondguessed, whereas only 45% of those from strong-execution organizations felt that way.

Recently, we worked with a global charitable organization dedicated to alleviating poverty. It had a problem others might envy: It was suffering from the strain brought on by a rapid growth in donations and a corresponding increase in the depth and breadth of ist program offerings. As you might expect, this nonprofit was populated with people on a mission who took intense personal ownership of projects. It did not reward the delegation of even the most mundane administrative tasks. Country-level managers, for example, would personally oversee copier repairs. Managers' inability to delegate led to decision paralysis and a lack of accountability as the organization grew. Second-guessing was an art form. When there was doubt over who was empowered to make a decision, the default was often to have a series of meetings in which no decision was reached. When decisions were finally made, they had generally been vetted by so many parties that no one person could be held accountable. An effort to expedite decision-making through restructuring—by collocating key leaders with subject-matter experts in newly established central and regional centers of excellence— became instead another logjam. Key managers still weren't sure of their right to take advantage of these centers, so they didn't.

The nonprofit's management and directors went back to the drawing board. We worked with them to design a decision-making map, a tool to help identify where different types of decisions should be taken, and with it they clarified and enhanced decision rights at all levels of management. All managers were then actively encouraged to delegate standard operational tasks. Once people had a clear idea of what decisions they should and should not be making, holding them accountable for decisions felt fair. What's more, now they could focus their energies on the organization's mission. Clarifying decision rights and responsibilities also improved the organization's ability to track individual achievement, which helped it chart new and appealing career-advancement paths.

4. Information flows freely across organizational boundaries. When information does not flow horizontally across different parts of the company, units behave like silos, forfeiting economies of scale and the transfer of best practices. Moreover, the organization as a whole loses the opportunity to develop a cadre of up-and-coming managers well versed in all aspects of the company's operations. Our research indicates that only 21% of respondents from weak-execution companies thought information flowed freely across organizational boundaries whereas 55% of those from strongexecution firms did. Since scores for even the strong companies are pretty low, though, this is an issue that most companies can work on.businessto-business company whose customer and product teams failed to collaborate in serving a key segment: large, cross-product customers. To manage relationships with important clients, the company had established a customer-focused marketing group, which developed customer outreach programs, innovative pricing models, and tailored promotions and discounts. But this group issued no clear and consistent reports of its initiatives and progress to the product units and had difficulty securing time with the regular crossunit management to discuss key performance issues. Each product unit communicated and planned in its own way, and it took tremendous energy for the customer group to understand the units' various priorities and tailor communications to each one. So the units were not aware, and had little faith, that this new division was making constructive inroads into a key customer segment. Conversely (and predictably), the customer team felt the units paid only perfunctory attention to its plans and couldn't get their cooperation on issues critical to multiproduct customers, such as potential trade-offs and volume discounts.

Historically, this lack of collaboration hadn't been a problem because the company had been the dominant player in a high-margin market. But as the market became more competitive, customers began to view the firm as unreliable and, generally, as a difficult supplier, and they became increasingly reluctant to enter into favorable relationships.

Once the issues became clear, though, the solution wasn't terribly complicated, involving little more than getting the groups to talk to one another. The customer division became responsible for issuing regular reports to the product units showing performance against targets, by product and geographic region, and for supplying a supporting rootcause analysis. A standing performancemanagement meeting was placed on the schedule every quarter, creating a forum for exchanging information face-to-face and discussing outstanding issues. These moves bred the broader organizational trust required for collaboration.

5. Field and line employees usually have the information they need to understand the bottom-line impact of their day-to-day choices. Rational decisions are necessarily bounded by the information available to employees. If managers don't understand what it will cost to capture an incremental dollar in revenue, they will always pursue the incremental revenue. They can hardly be faulted, even if their decision is—in the light of full information—wrong. Our research shows that 61% of individuals in strong-execution organizations agree that field and line employees have the information they need to understand the bottom-line impact of their decisions. This figure plummets to 28% in weak-execution organizations.

We saw this unhealthy dynamic play out at a large, diversified financial-services client, which had been built through a series of successful mergers of small regional banks. In combining operations, managers had chosen to separate front-office bankers who sold loans from back-office support groups who did risk assessments, placing each in a different reporting relationship and, in many cases, in different locations. Unfortunately, they failed to institute the necessary information and motivation links to ensure smooth operations. As a result, each pursued different, and often competing, goals.

For example, salespeople would routinely enter into highly customized one-off deals with clients that cost the company more than they made in revenues. Sales did not have a clear understanding of the cost and complexity implications of these transactions. Without sufficient information, sales staff believed that the back-end people were sabotaging their deals, while the support groups considered the front-end people to be cowboys. At year's end, when the data were finally reconciled, management would bemoan the sharp increase in operational costs, which often erased the profit from these transactions.

Executives addressed this information misalignment by adopting a "smart customization" approach to sales. They standardized the end-to-end processes used in the majority of deals and allowed for customization only in select circumstances. For these customized deals, they established clear back-office processes and analytical support tools to arm salespeople with accurate information on the cost implications of the proposed transactions. At the same time, they rolled out common reporting standards and tools for both the front- and back-office operations to ensure that each group had access to the same data and metrics when making decisions. Once each side understood the business realities confronted by the other, they cooperated more effectively, acting in the whole company's best interests and there were no more year-end surprises.

Creating a Transformation Program. The four building blocks that managers can use to improve strategy execution—decision rights, information, structure, and motivators are inextricably linked. Unclear decision rights not only paralyze decision making but also impede information flow, divorce performance from rewards, and prompt workarounds that subvert formal reporting lines. Blocking information results in poor decisions, limited career development, and a reinforcement of structural silos. So what to do about it?

Since each organization is different and faces a unique set of internal and external variables, there is no universal answer to that question. The first step is to identify the sources of the problem. In our work, we often begin by having a company's employees take our profiling survey and consolidating the results. The more people in the organization who take the survey, the better.

Once executives understand their company's areas of weakness, they can take any number of actions. The exhibit, "Mapping Improvements to the Building Blocks: Some Sample Tactics" shows 15 possible steps that can have an impact on performance. (The options listed represent only a sampling of the dozens of choices managers might make.) All of these actions are geared toward strengthening one or more of the 17 traits. For example, if you were to take steps to "clarify and streamline decision making" you could potentially strengthen two traits: "Everyone has a good idea of the decisions and actions for which he or she is responsible," and "Once made, decisions are rarely second-guessed."

You certainly wouldn't want to put 15 initiativesin a single transformation program. Most organizations don't have the managerial capacity or organizational appetite to take on more than five or six at a time. And as we've stressed, you should first take steps to address decision rights and information, and then design the necessary changes to motivators and structure to support the new design.

To help companies understand their shortcomings and construct the improvement program that will have the greatest impact, we have developed an organizational-change simulator. This interactive tool accompanies the profiler, allowing you to try out different elements of a change program virtually, to see which ones will best target your company's particular area of weakness.

To get a sense of the process from beginning to end—from taking the diagnostic profiler, to formulating your strategy, to launching your organizational transformation—consider the experience of a leading insurance company we'll call Goodward Insurance. Goodward was a successful company with strong capital reserves and steady revenue and customer growth. Still, its leadership wanted to further enhance execution to deliver on an ambitious five-year strategic agenda that included aggressive targets in customer growth, revenue increases, and cost reduction, which would require a new level of teamwork. While there were pockets of cross-unit collaboration within the company, it was far more common for each unit to focus on its own goals, making it difficult to spare resources to support another unit's goals. In many cases there was little incentive to do so anyway: Unit A's goals might require the involvement of Unit B to succeed, but Unit B's goals might not include supporting Unit A's effort.

The company had initiated a number of enterprisewide projects over the years, which had been completed on time and on budget, but these often had to be reworked because stakeholder needs hadn't been sufficiently taken into account. After launching a sharedservices center, for example, the company had to revisit its operating model and processes when units began hiring shadow staff to focus on priority work that the center wouldn't expedite. The center might decide what technology applications, for instance, to develop on its own rather than set priorities according to what was most important to the organization.

In a similar way, major product launches were hindered by insufficient coordination among departments. The marketing department would develop new coverage options without asking the claims-processing group whether it had the ability to process the claims. Since it didn't, processors had to create expensive manual work-arounds when the new kinds of claims started pouring in. Nor did marketing ask the actuarial department how these products would affect the risk profile and reimbursement expenses of the company, and for some of the new products, costs did indeed increase.

To identify the greatest barriers to building a stronger execution culture, Goodward Insurance gave the diagnostic survey to all of ist 7,000-plus employees and compared the organization's scores on the 17 traits with those from strong-execution companies. Numerous previous surveys (employee-satisfaction, among others) had elicited qualitative comments identifying the barriers to execution excellence. But the diagnostic survey gave the company quantifiable data that it could analyze by group and by management level to determine which barriers were most hindering the people actually charged with execution. As it turned out, middle management was far more pessimistic than the top executives in their assessment of the organization's execution ability. Their input became especially critical to the change agenda ultimately adopted.

Through the survey, Goodward Insurance uncovered impediments to execution in three of the most influential organizational traits:

Information did not flow freely across organizational boundaries. Sharing information was never one of Goodward's hallmarks, but managers had always dismissed the mounting anecdotal evidence of poor cross-divisional information flow as "some other group's problem." The organizational diagnostic data, however, exposed such plausible deniability as an inadequate excuse. In fact, when the CEO reviewed the profiler results with his direct reports, he held up the chart on cross-group information flows and declared, "We've been discussing this problem for several years, and yet you always say that it's so-and-so's problem, not mine. Sixty-seven percent of [our] respondents said that they do not think information flows freely across divisions. This is not so-and-so's problem it's our problem. You just don't get results that low [unless it comes] from everywhere. We are all on the hook for fixing this."

Contributing to this lack of horizontal information flow was a dearth of lateral promotions. Because Goodward had always promoted up rather than over and up, most middle and senior managers remained within a single group. They were not adequately apprised of the activities of the other groups, nor did they have a network of contacts across the organization.

Important information about the competitive environment did not get to headquarters quickly. The diagnostic data and subsequent surveys and interviews with middle management revealed that the wrong information was moving up the org chart. Mundane day-to-day decisions were escalated to the executive level—the top team had to approve midlevel hiring decisions, for instance, and bonuses of $1,000—limiting Goodward's agility in responding to competitors' moves, customers' needs, and changes in the broader marketplace. Meanwhile, more important information was so heavily filtered as it moved up the hierarchy that it was all but worthless for rendering key verdicts. Even if lower-level managers knew that a certain project could never work for highly valid reasons, they would not communicate that dim view to the top team. Nonstarters not only started, they kept going. For instance, the company had a project under way to create new incentives for its brokers. Even though this approach had been previously tried without success, no one spoke up in meetings or stopped the project because it was a priority for one of the top-team members.

No one had a good idea of the decisions and actions for which he or she was responsible. The general lack of information flow extended to decision rights, as few managers understood where their authority ended and another's began. Accountability even for dayto-day decisions was unclear, and managers did not know whom to ask for clarification. Naturally, confusion over decision rights led to second-guessing. Fifty-five percent of respondents felt that decisions were regularly second-guessed at Goodward.

To Goodward's credit, its top executives immediately responded to the results of the diagnostic by launching a change program targeted at all three problem areas. The program integrated early, often symbolic, changes with longer-term initiatives, in an effort to build momentum and galvanize participation and ownership. Recognizing that a passive-aggressive attitude toward people perceived to be in power solely as a result of their position in the hierarchy was hindering information flow, they took immediate steps to signal their intention to create a more informal and open culture. One symbolic change: the seating at management meetings was rearranged. The top executives used to sit in a separate section, the physical space between them and the rest of the room fraught with symbolism. Now they intermingled, making themselves more accessible and encouraging people to share information informally. Regular brown-bag lunches were established with members of the C-suite, where people had a chance to discuss the overall culture-change initiative, decision rights, new mechanisms for communicating across the units, and so forth. Seating at these events was highly choreographed to ensure that a mix of units was represented at each table. Icebreaker activities were designed to encourage individuals to learn about other units'work.

Meanwhile, senior managers commenced the real work of remedying issues relating to information flows and decision rights. They assessed their own informal networks to understand how people making key decisions got their information, and they identified critical gaps. The outcome was a new framework for making important decisions that clearly specifies who owns each decision, who must provide input, who is ultimately accountable for the results, and how results are defined. Other longer-term initiatives include:

- Pushing certain decisions down into the organization to better align decision rights with the best available information. Most hiring and bonus decisions, for instance, have been delegated to immediate managers, so long as they are within preestablished boundaries relating to numbers hired and salary levels. Being clear about who needs what information is encouraging cross-group dialogue.

- Identifying and eliminating duplicative committees.

- Pushing metrics and scorecards down to the group level, so that rather than focus on solving the mystery of who caused a problem, management can get right to the root cause of why the problem occurred. A well-designed scorecard captures not only outcomes (like sales volume or revenue) but also leading indicators of those outcomes (such as the number of customer calls or completed customer plans). As a result, the focus of management conversations has shifted from trying to explain the past to charting the future anticipating and preventing problems.

- Making the planning process more inclusive. Groups are explicitly mapping out the ways their initiatives depend on and affect one another; shared group goals are assigned accordingly.

The Secrets to Successful Strategy Execution

•Enhancing the middle management career path to emphasize the importance of lateral moves to career advancement.

- ▦ Focus corporate staff on supporting business-unit decision making.
- ▦ Clarify and streamline decision making at each operating level.
- ▦ Focus headquarters on important strategic questions.
- ▦ Create centers of excellence by consolidating similar functions into a single organizational unit.
- ▦ Assign process owners to coordinate activities that span organizational functions.
- ▦ Establish individual performance measures.
- Improve field-to-headquarters information flow.
- Define and distribute daily operating metrics to the field or line.
- Create cross-functional teams.
- Introduce differentiating performance awards.
- Expand nonmonetary rewards to recognize exceptional performers.
- ▦ Increase position tenure.
- ▦ Institute lateral moves and rotations.
- ▦ Broaden spans of control.

BUILDING BLOCKS ▦ Decision Rights   Information | Motivators ▦ Structure

Goodward Insurance has just embarked on this journey. The insurer has distributed ownership of these initiatives among various groups and management levels so that these efforts don't become silos in themselves. Already, solid improvement in the company's execution is beginning to emerge. The early evidence of success has come from employeesatisfaction surveys: Middle management responses to the questions about levels of cross-unit collaboration and clarity of decision making have improved as much as 20 to 25 percentage points. And high performers are already reaching across boundaries to gain a broader understanding of the full business, even if it doesn't mean a better title right away.

Orious and perennial challenge. Even at the companies that are best at it what we call "resilient organizations" just two-thirds of employees agree that important strategic and operational decisions are quickly translated into action. As long as companies continue to attack their execution problems primarily or solely with structural or motivational initiatives, they will continue to fail. As we've seen, they may enjoy short-term results, but they will

49

inevitably slip back into old habits because they won't have addressed the root causes of failure. Such failures can almost always be fixed by ensuring that people truly understand what they are responsible for and who makes which decisions—and then giving them the information they need to fulfill their responsibilities. With these two building blocks in place, structural and motivational elements will follow.

Mapping Improvements to the Building Blocks: Some Sample Tactics. Companies can take a host of steps to improve their ability to execute strategy. The 15 here are only some of the possible examples. Every one strengthens one or more of the building blocks executives can use to improve their strategy-execution capability: clarifying decision rights, improving information, establishing the right motivators, and restructuring the organization.

Test-Drive Your Organization's Transformation. You know your organization could perform better. You are faced with dozens of levers you could conceivably pull if you had unlimited time and resources. But you don't. You operate in the real world.

How, then, do you make the most-educated and cost-efficient decisions about which change initiatives to implement? We've developed a way to test the efficacy of specific actions (such as clarifying decision rights, forming cross-functional teams, or expanding nonmonetary rewards) without risking significant amounts of time and money. You can go to www.simulator-orgeffectiveness.com to assemble and try out various five-step organizational-change programs and assess which would be the most effective and efficient in improving execution at your company.

You begin the simulation by selecting one of seven organizational profiles that most resembles the current state of your organization. If you're not sure, you can take a fiveminute diagnostic survey. This online survey automatically generates an organizational profile and baseline execution-effectiveness score. (Although 100 is a perfect score, nobody is perfect; even the most effective companies often score in the 60s and 70s.)

Having established your baseline, you use the simulator to chart a possible course you'd like to take to improve your execution capabilities by selecting five out of a possible 28 actions. Ideally, these moves should directly address the weakest links in your organizational profile. To help you make the right choices, the simulator offers insights that shed further light on how a proposed action influences particular organizational elements.

Once you have made your selections, the simulator executes the steps you've elected and processes them through a web-based engine that evaluates them using empirical relationships identified from 31 companies representing more than 26,000 data observations. It then generates a bar chart indicating how much your organization's execution score has improved and where it now stands in relation to the highest-performing companies from our research and the scores of other people like you who have used the simulator starting from the same original profile you did. If you wish, you may then advance to the next round and pick another five actions. What you will see is illustrated below.

The beauty of the simulator is its ability to consider—consequence-free—the impact on execution of endless combinations of possible actions. Each simulation includes only two rounds, but you can run the simulation as many times as you like. The simulator has also been used for team competition within organizations, and we've found that it engenders very engaging and productive dialogue among senior executives.

While the simulator cannot capture all of the unique situations an organization might face, it is a useful tool for assessing and building a targeted and effective organizationtransformation program. It serves as a vehicle to stimulate thinking about the impact of various changes, saving untold amounts of time and resources in the process.

The Idea in Brief

A brilliant strategy may put you on the competitive map. But only solid execution keeps you there. Unfortunately, most companies struggle with implementation. That's because they overrely on structural changes, such as reorganization, to execute their strategy.

Though structural change has its place in execution, it produces only short-term gains. For example, one company reduced its management layers as part of a strategy to address disappointing performance. Costs plummeted initially, but the layers soon crept back in.

Research by Neilson, Martin, and Powers shows that execution exemplars focus their efforts on two levers far more powerful than structural change:

- Clarifying decision rights—for instance, specifying who "owns" each decision and who must provide input

- Ensuring information flows where it's needed— such as promoting managers laterally so they build networks needed for the cross-unit collaboration critical to a new strategy

Tackle decision rights and information flows first, and only then alter organizational structures and realign incentives to *support* those moves.

The following levers matter *most* for successful strategy execution:

DECISION RIGHTS

- Ensure that everyone in your company knows which decisions and actions they're responsible for.

Example: In one global consumer-goods company, decisions made by divisional and geographic leaders were overridden by corporate functional

leaders who controlled resource allocations. Decisions stalled. Overhead costs mounted as divisions added staff to create bulletproof cases for challenging corporate decisions. To support a new strategy hinging on sharper customer focus, the CEO designated accountability for profits unambiguously to the divisions.

- Encourage higher-level managers to delegate operational decisions.

Example: At one global charitable organization, country-level managers' inability to delegate led to decision paralysis. So the leadership team encouraged country managers to delegate standard operational tasks. This freed these managers to focus on developing the strategies needed to fulfill the organization's mission.

INFORMATION FLOW

- Make sure important information about the competitive environment flows quickly to corporate headquarters. That way, the top team can identify patterns and promulgate best practices throughout the company.

Example: At one insurance company, accurate information about projects' viability was censored as it moved up the hierarchy. To improve information flow to senior levels of management, the company took steps to create a more open, informal culture. Top executives began mingling with unit leaders during management meetings and held regular brown-bag lunches where people discussed the company's most pressing issues.

- Facilitate information flow across organizational boundaries.

Example: To better manage relationships with large, cross-product customers, a B2B company needed its units to talk with one another. It charged its newly created customer-focused marketing group with encouraging cross-company communication. The group issued regular reports showing performance against targets (by product and geography) and supplied root-cause analyses of performance gaps. Quarterly performance-management meetings further fostered the trust required for collaboration.

- Help field and line employees understand how their day-to-day choices affect your company's bottom line.

Example: At a financial services firm, salespeople routinely crafted customized one-off deals with clients that cost the company more than it made in revenues. Sales didn't understand the cost and complexity implications of these transactions. Management addressed the information misalignment by adopting a "smart customization" approach to sales. For customized deals, it established standardized back-office processes (such as risk assessment). It also developed analytical support tools to arm salespeople with accurate information on the cost implications of their proposed transactions. Profitability improved.

CHAPTER 4
Turning Great Strategy into Great Performance

Companies typically realize only about 60% of their strategies' potential value because of defects and breakdowns in planning and execution. By strictly following seven simple rules, you can get a lot more than that. by Michael C. Mankins and Richard Steele

Three years ago, the leadership team at a major manufacturer spent months developing a new strategy for its European business. Over the prior half-decade, six new competitors had entered the market, each deploying the latest in low-cost manufacturing technology and slashing prices to gain market share. The performance of the European unit—once the crown jewel of the company's portfolio—had deteriorated to the point that top management was seriously considering divesting it.

To turn around the operation, the unit's leadership team had recommended a bold new "solutions strategy"—one that would leverage the business's installed base to fuel growth in after-market services and equipment financing. The financial forecasts were exciting—the strategy promised to restore the business's industry-leading returns and growth. Impressed, top management quickly approved the plan, agreeing to provide the unit with all the resources it needed to make the turnaround a reality.

Today, however, the unit's performance is nowhere near what its management team had projected. Returns, while better than before, remain well below the company's cost of capital. The revenues and profits that managers had expected from services and financing have not materialized, and the business's cost position still lags behind that of its major competitors.

At the conclusion of a recent half-day review of the business's strategy and performance, the unit's general manager remained steadfast and vowed to press on. "It's all about execution," she declared. "The strategy we're pursuing is the right one. We're just not delivering the numbers. All we need to do is work harder, work smarter."

The parent company's CEO was not so sure. He wondered: Could the unit's lackluster performance have more to do with a mistaken strategy than poor execution? More important, what should he do to get better performance out of the unit? Should he do as the general manager insisted and stay the course focusing the organization more intensely on execution—or should he encourage the leadership team to investigate new strategy options? If execution was the issue, what should he do to help the business improve its game? Or should he just cut his losses and sell the business? He left the operating review frustrated and confused—not at all confident that the business would ever deliver the performance its managers had forecast in its strategic plan.

Talk to almost any CEO, and you're likely to hear similar frustrations. For despite the enormous time and energy that goes into strategy development at most companies, many have little to show for the effort. Our research suggests that companies on average deliver only 63% of the financial performance their strategies promise. Even worse, the causes of this strategy-to-performance gap are all but invisible to top management. Leaders then pull the wrong levers in their attempts to turn around performance—pressing for better execution when they actually need a better strategy, or opting to change direction when they really should focus the organization on execution. The result: wasted energy, lost time, and continued underperformance.

But, as our research also shows, a select group of high-performing companies have managed to close the strategy-to-performance gap through better planning *and* execution. These companies—Barclays, Cisco Systems, Dow Chemical, 3M, and Roche, to name a few—develop realistic plans that are solidly grounded in the underlying economics of their markets and then use the plans to drive execution. Their disciplined planning and execution processes make it far less likely that they will face a shortfall in actual performance. And, if they do fall short, their processes enable them to discern the cause quickly and take corrective action. While these companies' practices are broad in scope—ranging from unique forms of planning to integrated processes for deploying and tracking resources—our experience suggests that they can be applied by any business to help craft great plans and turn them into great performance.

The Strategy-to-Performance Gap. In the fall of 2004, our firm, Marakon Associates, in collaboration with the Economist Intelligence Unit, surveyed senior executives from 197 companies worldwide with sales exceeding $500 million. We wanted to see how successful companies are at translating their strategies into performance. Specifically, how effective are they at meeting the financial projections set forth in their strategic plans? And when they fall short, what are the most common causes, and what actions are most effective in closing the strategy-to-performance gap? Our findings were revealing—and troubling.

While the executives we surveyed compete in very different product markets and geographies, they share many concerns about planning and execution. Virtually all of them struggle to produce the financial performance forecasts in their long-range plans. Furthermore, the processes they use to develop plans and monitor performance make it difficult to discern whether the strategy-to-performance gap stems from poor planning, poor execution, both, or neither. Specifically, we discovered:

Companies rarely track performance against long-term plans. In our experience, less than 15% of companies make it a regular practice to go back and compare the business's results with the performance forecast for each unit in its prior years' strategic plans. As a result, top managers can't easily know whether the projections that underlie their capital-investment and portfolio-strategy decisions are in any way predictive of actual performance. More important, they risk embedding the same disconnect between results and forecasts in their future investment decisions. Indeed, the fact that so few companies routinely monitor actual versus planned performance may help explain why so many companies seem to pour good money after bad—continuing to fund losing strategies rather than searching for new and better options.

Multiyear results rarely meet projections. When companies do track performance relative to projections over a number of years, what commonly emerges is a picture one of our clients recently described as a series of "diagonal venetian blinds," where each year's performance projections, when viewed side by side, resemble venetian blinds hung diagonally. If things are going reasonably well, the starting point for each year's new "blind" may be a bit higher than the prior year's starting point, but rarely does performance match the prior year's projection. The obvious implication: year after year of underperformance relative to plan.

The venetian blinds phenomenon creates a number of related problems. First, because the plan's financial forecasts are unreliable, senior management cannot confidently tie capital approval to strategic planning. Consequently, strategy development and resource allocation become decoupled, and the annual operating plan (or budget) ends up driving the company's long-term investments and strategy. Second, portfolio management gets derailed. Without credible financial forecasts, top management cannot know whether a particular business is worth more to the company and its shareholders than to potential buyers. As a result, businesses that destroy shareholder value stay in the portfolio too long (in the hope that their performance will eventually turn around), and value-creating businesses are starved for capital and other resources. Third, poor financial forecasts complicate communications with the investment community. Indeed, to avoid coming up short at the end of the quarter, the CFO and head of investor relations frequently impose a "contingency" or "safety margin" on top of the forecast produced by consolidating the business-unit plans. Because this top-down contingency is wrong just as often as it is right, poor financial forecasts run the risk of damaging a company's reputation with analysts and investors.

A lot of value is lost in translation. Given the poor quality of financial forecasts in most strategic plans, it is probably not surprising that most   companies fail to realize their strategies' potential value. As we've mentioned, our survey indicates that, on average, most strategies deliver only 63% of their potential financial performance. And more than one-third of the executives surveyed placed the figure at less than 50%. Put differently, if management were to realize the full potential of its current strategy, the increase in value could be as much as 60% to 100%!

As illustrated in the exhibit "Where the Performance Goes," the strategy-to-performance gap can be attributed to a combination of factors, such as poorly formulated plans, misapplied resources, breakdowns in communication, and limited accountability for results. To elaborate, management starts with a strategy it believes will generate a certain level of financial performance and value over time (100%, as noted in the exhibit). But, according to the executives we surveyed, the failure to have the right resources in the right place at the right time strips away some 7.5% of the strategy's potential value. Some 5.2% is lost to poor communications, 4.5% to poor action planning, 4.1% to blurred accountabilities, and so on. Of course, these estimates reflect the average experience of the executives we surveyed and may not be representative of every company or every strategy. Nonetheless, they do highlight the issues managers need to focus on as they review their companies' processes for planning and executing strategies.

What emerges from our survey results is a sequence of events that goes something like this: Strategies are approved but poorly communicated. This, in turn, makes the translation of strategy into specific actions and resource plans all but impossible. Lower levels in the organization don't know what they need to do, when they need to do it, or what resources will be required to deliver the performance senior management expects. Consequently, the expected results never materialize. And because no one is held responsible for the shortfall, the cycle of underperformance gets repeated, often for many years.

Performance bottlenecks are frequently invisible to top management. The processes most companies use to develop plans, allocate resources, and track performance make it difficult for top management to discern whether the strategy-to-performance gap stems from poor planning, poor execution, both, or neither. Because so many plans incorporate overly ambitious projections, companies frequently write off performance shortfalls as "just another hockey-stick forecast." And when plans are realistic and performance falls short, executives have few early-warning signals. They often have no way of knowing whether critical actions were carried out as expected, resources were deployed on schedule, competitors responded as anticipated, and so on. Unfortunately, without clear information on how and why performance is falling short, it is virtually impossible for top management to take appropriate corrective action.

The strategy-to-performance gap fosters a culture of underperformance. In many companies, planning and execution breakdowns are reinforced—even magnified—by an insidious shift in culture. In our experience, this change occurs subtly but quickly, and once it has taken root it is very hard to reverse. First, unrealistic plans create the expectation throughout the organization that plans simply will not be fulfilled. Then, as the expectation becomes experience, it becomes the norm that performance commitments won't be kept. So commitments cease to be binding promises with real consequences. Rather than stretching to ensure that commitments are kept, managers, expecting failure, seek to protect themselves from the eventual fallout. They spend time covering their tracks rather than identifying actions to enhance performance. The organization becomes less self-critical and less intellectually honest about its shortcomings. Consequently, it loses its capacity to perform.

Closing the Strategy-to-Performance Gap. As significant as the strategy-to-performance gap is at most companies, management can close it. A number of high-performing companies have found ways to realize more of their strategies' potential. Rather than focus on improving their planning and execution processes separately to close the gap, these companies work both sides of the equation, raising standards for both planning and execution simultaneously and creating clear links between them.

Our research and experience in working with many of these companies suggests they follow seven rules that apply to planning and execution. Living by these rules enables them to objectively assess any performance shortfall and determine whether it stems from the strategy, the plan, the execution, or employees' capabilities. And the same rules that allow them to spot problems early also help them prevent performance shortfalls in the first place. These rules may seem simple—even obvious—but when strictly and collectively observed, they can transform both the quality of a company's strategy and its ability to deliver results.

Rule 1: Keep it simple, make it concrete. At most companies, strategy is a highly abstract concept—often confused with vision or aspiration—and is not something that can be easily communicated or translated into action. But without a clear sense of where the company is headed and why, lower levels in the organization cannot put in place executable plans. In short, the link between strategy and performance can't be drawn because the strategy itself is not sufficiently concrete.

To start off the planning and execution process on the right track, high-performing companies avoid long, drawn-out descriptions of lofty goals and instead stick to clear language describing their course of action. Bob Diamond, CEO of Barclays Capital, one of the fastestgrowing and best-performing investment banking operations in Europe, puts it this way: "We've been very clear about what we will and will not do. We knew we weren't going to go head-to-head with U.S. bulge bracket firms. We communicated that we wouldn't compete in this way and that we wouldn't play in unprofitable segments within the equity markets but instead would invest to position ourselves for the euro, the burgeoning need for fixed income, and the end of Glass-Steigel. By ensuring everyone knew the strategy and how it was different, we've been able to spend more time on tasks that are key to executing this strategy."

By being clear about what the strategy is and isn't, companies like Barclays keep everyone headed in the same direction. More important, they safeguard the performance their counterparts lose to ineffective communications; their resource and action planning becomes more effective; and accountabilities are easier to specify.

Rule 2: Debate assumptions, not forecasts. At many companies, a business unit's strategic plan is little more than a negotiated settlement—the result of careful bargaining with the corporate center over performance targets and financial forecasts. Planning, therefore, is largely a political process—with unit management arguing for lower near-term profit projections (to secure higher annual bonuses) and top management pressing for more long-term stretch (to satisfy the board of directors and other external constituents). Not surprisingly, the forecasts that emerge from these negotiations almost always understate what each business unit can deliver in the near term and overstate what can realistically be expected in the long-term—the hockey-stick charts with which CEOs are all too familiar.

Even at companies where the planning process is isolated from the political concerns of performance evaluation and compensation, the approach used to generate financial projections often has built-in biases. Indeed, financial forecasting frequently takes place in complete isolation from the marketing or strategy functions. A business unit's finance function prepares a highly detailed line-item forecast whose short-term assumptions may be realistic, if conservative, but whose longterm assumptions are largely uninformed. For example, revenue forecasts are typically based on crude estimates about average pricing, market growth, and market share. Projections of long-term costs and working capital requirements are based on an assumption about annual productivity gains—expediently tied, perhaps, to some companywide efficiency program. These forecasts are difficult for top management to pick apart. Each line item may be completely defensible, but the overall plan and projections embed a clear upward bias—rendering them useless for driving strategy execution.

High-performing companies view planning altogether differently. They want their forecasts to drive the work they actually do. To make this possible, they have to ensure that the assumptions underlying their long-term plans reflect both the real economics of their markets and the performance experience of the company relative to competitors. Tyco CEO Ed Breen, brought in to turn the company around in July 2002, credits a revamped planbuilding process for contributing to Tyco's dramatic recovery. When Breen joined the company, Tyco was a labyrinth of 42 business units and several hundred profit centers, built up over many years through countless acquisitions. Few of Tyco's businesses had complete plans, and virtually none had reliable financial forecasts.

To get a grip on the conglomerate's complex operations, Breen assigned cross-functional teams at each unit, drawn from strategy, marketing, and finance, to develop detailed information on the profitability of Tyco's primary markets as well as the product or service offerings, costs, and price positioning relative to the competition. The teams met with corporate executives biweekly during Breen's first six months to review and discuss the findings. These discussions focused on the assumptions that would drive each unit's long-term financial performance, not on the financial forecasts themselves. In fact, once assumptions about market trends were agreed on, it was relatively easy for Tyco's central finance function to prepare externally oriented and internally consistent forecasts for each unit.

Separating the process of building assumptions from that of preparing financial projections helps to ground the business unit–corporate center dialogue in economic reality. Units can't hide behind specious details, and corporate center executives can't push for unrealistic goals. What's more, the fact-based discussion resulting from this kind of approach builds trust between the top team and each unit and removes barriers to fast and effective execution. "When you understand the fundamentals and performance drivers in a detailed way," says Bob Diamond, "you can then step back, and you don't have to manage the details. The team knows which issues it can get on with, which it needs to flag to me, and which issues we really need to work out together."

Rule 3: Use a rigorous framework, speak a common language. To be productive, the dialogue between the corporate center and the business units about market trends and assumptions must be conducted within a rigorous framework. Many of the companies we advise use the concept of profit pools, which draws on the competition theories of Michael Porter and others. In this framework, a business's long-term financial performance is tied to the total profit pool available in each of the markets it serves and its share of each profit pool—which, in turn, is tied to the business's market share and relative profitability versus competitors in each market.

In this approach, the first step is for the corporate center and the unit team to agree on the size and growth of each profit pool. Fiercely competitive markets, such as pulp and paper or commercial airlines, have small (or negative) total profit pools. Less competitive markets, like soft drinks or pharmaceuticals, have large total profit pools. We find it helpful to estimate the size of each profit pool directly through detailed benchmarking and then forecast changes in the pool's size and growth. Each business unit then assesses what share of the total profit pool it can realistically capture over time, given its business model and positioning. Competitively advantaged businesses can capture a large share of the profit pool—by gaining or sustaining a high market share, generating above-average profitability, or both. Competitively disadvantaged businesses, by contrast, typically capture a negligible share of the profit pool. Once the unit and the corporate center agree on the likely share of the pool the business will capture over time, the corporate center can easily create the financial projections that will serve as the unit's road map.

In our view, the specific framework a company uses to ground its strategic plans isn't all that important. What is critical is that the framework establish a common language for the dialogue between the corporate center and the units—one that the strategy, marketing, and finance teams all understand and use. Without a rigorous framework to link a busi ness's performance in the product markets with its financial performance over time, it is very difficult for top management to ascertain whether the financial projections that accompany a business unit's strategic plan are reasonable and realistically achievable. As a result, management can't know with confidence whether a performance shortfall stems from poor execution or an unrealistic and ungrounded plan.

Rule 4: Discuss resource deployments early. Companies can create more realistic forecasts and more executable plans if they discuss up front the level and timing of critical resource deployments. At Cisco Systems, for example, a cross-functional team reviews the level and timing of resource deployments early in the planning stage. These teams regularly meet with John Chambers (CEO), Dennis Powell (CFO), Randy Pond (VP of operations), and the other members of Cisco's executive team to discuss their findings and make recommendations. Once agreement is reached on resource allocation and timing at the unit level, those elements are factored into the company's two-year plan. Cisco then monitors each unit's actual resource deployments on a monthly basis (as well as its performance) to make sure things are going according to plan and that the plan is generating the expected results.

Challenging business units about when new resources need to be in place focuses the planning dialogue on what actually needs to happen across the company in order to execute each unit's strategy. Critical questions invariably surface, such as: How long will it take us to change customers' purchase patterns? How fast can we deploy our new sales force? How quickly will competitors respond? These are tough questions. But answering them makes the forecasts and the plans they accompany more feasible.

What's more, an early assessment of resource needs also informs discussions about market trends and drivers, improving the quality of the strategic plan and making it far more executable. In the course of talking about the resources needed to expand in the rapidly growing cable market, for example, Cisco came to realize that additional growth would require more trained engineers to improve existing products and develop new features. So, rather than relying on the functions to provide these resources from the bottom up, corporate management earmarked a specific number of trained engineers to support growth in cable. Cisco's financial-planning organization carefully monitors the engineering head count, the pace of feature development, and revenues generated by the business to make sure the strategy stays on track.

Rule 5: Clearly identify priorities. To deliver any strategy successfully, managers must make thousands of tactical decisions and put them into action. But not all tactics are equally important. In most instances, a few key steps must be taken—at the right time and in the right way—to meet planned performance. Leading companies make these priorities explicit so that each executive has a clear sense of where to direct his or her efforts.

At Textron, a $10 billion multi-industrial conglomerate, each business unit identifies "improvement priorities" that it must act upon to realize the performance outlined in its strategic plan. Each improvement priority is translated into action items with clearly defined accountabilities, timetables, and key performance indicators (KPIs) that allow executives to tell how a unit is delivering on a priority. Improvement priorities and action items cascade to every level at the company from the management committee (consisting of Textron's top five executives) down to the lowest levels in each of the company's ten business units. Lewis Campbell, Textron's CEO, summarizes the company's approach this way: "Everyone needs to know: 'If I have only one hour to work, here's what I'm going to focus on.' Our goal deployment process makes each individual's accountabilities and priorities clear."

The Swiss pharmaceutical giant Roche goes as far as to turn its business plans into detailed performance contracts that clearly specify the steps needed and the risks that must be managed to achieve the plans. These contracts all include a "delivery agenda" that lists the five to ten critical priorities with the greatest impact on performance. By maintaining a delivery agenda at each level of the company, Chairman and CEO Franz Humer and his leadership team make sure "everyone at Roche understands exactly what we have agreed to do at a strategic level and that our strategy gets translated into clear execution priorities. Our delivery agenda helps us stay the course with the strategy decisions we have made so that execution is actually allowed to happen. We cannot control implementation from HQ, but we can agree on the priorities, communicate relentlessly, and hold managers accountable for executing against their commitments."

Rule 6: Continuously monitor performance. Seasoned executives know almost instinctively whether a business has asked for too much, too little, or just enough resources to deliver the goods. They develop this capability over time—essentially through trial and error. High-performing companies use real-time performance tracking to help accelerate this trialand error process. They continuously monitor their resource deployment patterns and their results against plan, using continuous feedback to reset planning assumptions and reallocate resources. This real-time information allows management to spot and remedy flaws in the plan and shortfalls in execution—and to avoid confusing one with the other.

At Textron, for example, each KPI is carefully monitored, and regular operating reviews percolate performance shortfalls—or "red light" events—up through the management ranks. This provides CEO Lewis Campbell, CFO Ted French, and the other members of Textron's management committee with the information they need to spot and fix breakdowns in execution.

A similar approach has played an important role in the dramatic revival of Dow Chemical's fortunes. In December 2001, with performance in a free fall, Dow's board of directors asked Bill Stavropoulos (Dow's CEO from 1993 to 1999) to return to the helm. Stavropoulos and Andrew Liveris (the current CEO, then COO) immediately focused Dow's entire top leadership team on execution through a project they called the Performance Improvement Drive. They began by defining clear performance metrics for each of Dow's 79 business units. Performance on these key metrics was tracked against plans on a weekly basis, and the entire leadership team discussed any serious discrepancies first thing every Monday morning. As Liveris told us, the weekly monitoring sessions "forced everyone to live the details of execution" and let "the entire organization know how we were performing."

Continuous monitoring of performance is particularly important in highly volatile industries, where events outside anyone's control can render a plan irrelevant. Under CEO Alan Mulally, Boeing Commercial Airplanes' leadership team holds weekly business performance reviews to track the division's results against its multiyear plan. By tracking the deployment of resources as a leading indicator of whether a plan is being executed effectively, BCA's leadership team can make course corrections each week rather than waiting for quarterly results to roll in.

Furthermore, by proactively monitoring the primary drivers of performance (such as passenger traffic patterns, airline yields and load factors, and new aircraft orders), BCA is better able to develop and deploy effective countermeasures when events throw its plans off course. During the SARS epidemic in late 2002, for example, BCA's leadership team took action to mitigate the adverse consequences of the illness on the business's operating plan within a week of the initial outbreak. The abrupt decline in air traffic to Hong Kong, Singapore, and other Asian business centers signaled that the number of future aircraft deliveries to the region would fall—perhaps precipitously. Accordingly, BCA scaled back its medium-term production plans (delaying the scheduled ramp-up of some programs and accelerating the shutdown of others) and adjusted its multiyear operating plan to reflect the anticipated financial impact.

Rule 7: Reward and develop execution capabilities. No list of rules on this topic would be complete without a reminder that companies have to motivate and develop their staffs; at the end of the day, no process can be better than the people who have to make it work. Unsurprisingly, therefore, nearly all of the companies we studied insisted that the selection and development of management was an essential ingredient in their success. And while improving the capabilities of a company's workforce is no easy task—often taking many years—these capabilities, once built, can drive superior planning and execution for decades.

For Barclays' Bob Diamond, nothing is more important than "ensuring that [the company] hires only A players." In his view, "the hidden costs of bad hiring decisions are enormous, so despite the fact that we are doubling in size, we insist that as a top team we take responsibility for all hiring. The jury of your peers is the toughest judgment, so we vet each others' potential hires and challenge each other to keep raising the bar." It's equally important to make sure that talented hires are rewarded for superior execution. To reinforce its core values of "client," "meritocracy," "team," and "integrity," Barclays Capital has innovative pay schemes that "ring fence" rewards. Stars don't lose out just because the business is entering new markets with lower returns during the growth phase. Says Diamond: "It's so bad for the culture if you don't deliver what you promised to people who have delivered…. You've got to make sure you are consistent and fair, unless you want to lose your most productive people."

Companies that are strong on execution also emphasize development. Soon after he became CEO of 3M, Jim McNerney and his top team spent 18 months hashing out a new leadership model for the company. Challenging debates among members of the top team led to agreement on six "leadership attributes" namely, the ability to "chart the course," "energize and inspire others," "demonstrate ethics, integrity, and compliance," "deliver results," "raise the bar," and "innovate resourcefully." 3M's leadership agreed that these six attributes were essential for the company to become skilled at execution and known for accountability. Today, the leaders credit this model with helping 3M to sustain and even improve its consistently strong performance.

The prize for closing the strategy-to-performance gap is huge—an increase in performance of anywhere from 60% to 100% for most companies. But this almost certainly understates the true benefits. Companies that create tight links between their strategies, their plans, and, ultimately, their performance often experience a cultural multiplier effect. Over time, as they turn their strategies into great performance, leaders in these organizations become much more confident in their own capabilities and much more willing to make the stretch commitments that inspire and transform large companies. In turn, individual managers who keep their commitments are rewarded—with faster progression and fatter paychecks—reinforcing the behaviors needed to drive any company forward.

Eventually, a culture of overperformance emerges. Investors start giving management the benefit of the doubt when it comes to bold moves and performance delivery. The result is a performance premium on the company's stock—one that further rewards stretch commitments and performance delivery. Before long, the company's reputation among potential recruits rises, and a virtuous circle is created in which talent begets performance, performance begets rewards, and rewards beget even more talent. In short, closing the strategyto-performance gap is not only a source of immediate performance improvement but also an important driver of cultural change with a large and lasting impact on the organization's capabilities, strategies, and competitiveness.

The Venetian Blinds of Business. This graphic illustrates a dynamic common to many companies. In January 2001, management approves a strategic plan (Plan 2001) that projects modest performance for the first year and a high rate of performance thereafter, as shown in the first solid line. For beating the first year's projection, the unit management is both commended and handsomely rewarded. A new plan is then prepared, projecting uninspiring results for the first year and once again promising a

fast rate of performance improvement thereafter, as shown by the second solid line (Plan 2002). This, too, succeeds only partially, so another plan is drawn up, and so on. The actual rate of performance improvement can be seen by joining the start points of each plan (the dotted line).

The Idea in Brief

Most companies' strategies deliver only 63% of their promised financial value. Why? Leaders press for better execution when they really need a sounder strategy. Or they craft a new strategy when execution is the true weak spot.

How to avoid these errors? View strategic planning and execution as inextricably linked—then raise the bar for both simultaneously. Start by applying seven deceptively straightforward rules, including: keeping your strategy simple and concrete, making resource-allocation decisions early in the planning process, and continuously monitoring performance as you roll out your strategic plan.

By following these rules, you reduce the likelihood of performance shortfalls. And even if your strategy still stumbles, you quickly determine whether the fault lies with the strategy itself, your plan for pursuing it, or the execution process. The payoff? You make the *right* midcourse corrections promptly. And as high-performing companies like Cisco Systems, Dow Chemical, and 3M have discovered, you boost your company's financial performance 60% to 100%.

Seven rules for successful strategy execution:

- Keep it simple. Avoid drawn-out descriptions of lofty goals. Instead, clearly describe what your company will and won't do.

- Example: Executives at European investment-banking giant Barclays Capital stated they wouldn't compete with large U.S. investment banks or in unprofitable equitymarket segments. Instead, they'd position Barclays for investors' burgeoning need for fixed income.

- Challenge assumptions. Ensure that the assumptions underlying your long-term strategic plans reflect real market economics and your organization's actual performance relative to rivals'.

- Example: Struggling conglomerate Tyco commissioned cross-functional teams in each business unit to continuously analyze their markets' profitability and their offerings, costs, and price positioning relative to competitors'.

- Teams met with corporate executives biweekly to discuss their findings. The revamped process generated more realistic plans and contributed to Tyco's dramatic turnaround.

- Speak the same language. Unit leaders and corporate strategy, marketing, and finance teams must agree on a common framework for assessing performance. For example, some high-performing companies use benchmarking to estimate the size of the profit pool available in each market their company serves, the pool's potential growth, and the company's likely portion of that pool, given its market share and profitability. By using the shared approach, executives easily agree on financial projections.

- Discuss resource deployments early. Challenge business units about when they'll need new resources to execute their strategy. By asking questions such as, "How fast can you deploy the new sales force?" and "How quickly will competitors respond?" you create more feasible forecasts and plans.

- Identify priorities. Delivering planned performance requires a few key actions taken at the right time, in the right way. Make strategic priorities explicit, so everyone knows what to focus on.

- Continuously monitor performance. Track real-time results against your plan, resetting planning assumptions and reallocating resources as needed. You'll remedy flaws in your plan *and* its execution—and avoid confusing the two.

- Develop execution ability. No strategy can be better than the people who must implement it. Make selection and development of managers a priority.

Example: Barclays' top executive team takes responsibility for all hiring. Members vet each others' potential hires and reward talented newcomers for superior execution. And stars aren't penalized if their business enters new markets with lower initial returns.

CHAPTER 5

Transforming Corner-Office Strategy into Frontline Action

It's a challenge that confronts every company, large and small: how do you give employees clear strategic direction but also inspire flexibility and risk taking? One answer is to create and broadcast a "strategic principle"—a pithy, memorable distillation of strategy that guides employees as it empowers them. by Orit Gadiesh and James L. Gilbert

We all know the benefits of pushing decision making from the CEO's office out to the far reaches of an organization. Fleeting business opportunities can be seized quickly. Products and services better reflect subtle shifts in customers' preferences. Empowered workers are motivated to innovate and take risks.

But while the value of such an approach is clear, particularly in a volatile business environment, there is also a built-in risk: an organization in which everyone is a decision maker has the potential to spin out of control. Within a single company, it's tricky to achieve both decentralized decision making and coherent strategic action. Still, some companies—think General Electric, America Online, Vanguard, Dell, Wal-Mart, Southwest Airlines, and eBay—have done just that.

These companies employ what we call a *strategic principle,* a memorable and actionable phrase that distills a company's corporate strategy into its unique essence and communicates it throughout the organization. (For a list of companies' strategic principles.)

This tool—which we have observed in use at about a dozen companies, even though they don't label it as such—would always serve a company well. But it has become particularly useful in today's rapidly and constantly changing business environment. Indeed, in our conversations and work with more than 50 CEOs over the past two years, we have come to appreciate the strategic principle's power—its ability to help companies maintain strategic focus while fostering the flexibility among employees that permits innovation and a rapid response to opportunities. Strategic principles are likely to become even more crucial to corporate success in the years ahead.

Distillation and Communication. To better understand what a strategic principle is and how it can be used, it may be helpful to look at a military analogy: the rules of engagement for battle. For example, Admiral Lord Nelson's crews in Britain's eighteenthcentury wars against the French were guided by a simple strategic principle: whatever you do, get alongside an enemy ship.

The Royal Navy's seamanship, training, and experience gave it the advantage every time it engaged one-on-one against any of Europe's lesser fleets. So Nelson rejected as impractical the common practice of an admiral attempting to control a fleet through the use of flag signals. Instead, he gave his captains strategic parameters—they knew they had to battle rival ships one-on-one—leaving them to determine exactly how to engage in such combat. By using a strategic principle instead of explicit signals to direct his forces, Nelson consistently defeated the French, including a great victory in the dark of night, when signals would have been useless. Nelson's rule of engagement was simple enough for every one of his officers and sailors to know by heart. And it was enduring, a valid directive that was good until the relative naval capabilities of Britain and its rivals changed.

The distillation of a company's strategy into a pithy, memorable, and prescriptive phrase is important because a brilliant business strategy, like an insightful approach to warfare, is of little use unless people understand it well enough to apply it—both to anticipated decisions and unforeseen opportunities. In our work, we often see evidence of what we call the 80-100 rule: you're better off with a strategy that is 80% right and 100% implemented than one that is 100% right but doesn't drive consistent action throughout the company. A strategic principle can help a company balance that ratio.

The beauty of having a corporate strategic principle—a company should have only one—is that everyone in an organization, the executives in the front office as well as people in the operating units, can knowingly work toward the same strategic objective without being rigid about how they do so. Decisions don't always have to make the slow trip to and from the executive suite. When a strategic principle is well crafted and effectively communicated, managers at all levels can be trusted to make decisions that advance rather than undermine company strategy.

Given what we've said so far, a strategic principle might seem to be a mission statement by another name. But while both help employees understand a company's direction, the two are different tools that communicate different things. A mission statement informs a company's *culture*. A strategic principle drives a company's *strategy*. A mission statement is *aspirational*: it gives people something to strive for. A strategic principle is *action oriented*: it enables people to do something now. A mission statement is meant to *inspire* frontline workers. A strategic principle enables them to *act* quickly by giving them explicit guidance to make strategically consistent choices.

Consider the difference between GE's mission statement and its strategic principle. The company's mission statement exhorts GE's leaders—"always with unyielding integrity"—to be "passionately focused on driving customer success" and to "create an environment of 'stretch,' excitement, informality, and trust," among other things. The language is aspirational and emotional. By contrast, GE's wellknown strategic principle—"Be number one or number two in every industry in which we compete, or get out"—is action oriented. The first part of the phrase is an explicit strategic challenge, and the second part leaves no question in line managers' minds about what they should do.

Three Defining Attributes. A strategic principle, as the distillation of a company's strategy, should guide a company's allocation of scarce resources—capital, time, management's attention, labor, and brand—in order to build a sustainable competitive advantage. It should tell a company what to do and, just as important, what not to do. More specifically, an effective strategic principle does the following:

- It forces trade-offs between competing resource demands;

- It tests the strategic soundness of a particular action;

- It sets clear boundaries within which employees must operate while granting them freedom to experiment within those constraints.

These three qualities can be seen in America Online's strategic principle. CEO Steve Case says personal interaction on-line is the soul of the Internet, and he has positioned AOL to create that interaction. Thus, AOL's strategic principle in the years leading up to its recent merger with Time Warner has been "Consumer connectivity first—anytime, anywhere."

This strategic principle has helped AOL make tough choices when allocating its re sources. For example, in 1997, the company needed cash to grow, so it sold off its network infrastructure and outsourced that capability a risky move at a time when it appeared that network ownership might be the key to success on the Internet. In keeping with its strategic principle, AOL instead spent its time and cash on improving connectivity at its Web site, focusing particularly on access, navigation, and interaction. As a result, it avoided investing capital in what turned out to be a relatively low-return business.

Its strategic principle has also helped AOL test whether a given business move makes strategic sense. For instance, the Internet company has chosen to expand its global network through alliances with local partners, even though that approach can take longer than simply transplanting AOL's own technology and know-how. AOL acknowledges that a local partner better understands the native culture and community, which is essential for connecting with customers.

Finally, AOL's strategic principle has spurred focused experimentation in the field by clearly defining employees' latitude for making moves. For example, AOL's former vice president of marketing, Jan Brandt, mailed more than 250 million AOL diskettes to consumers nationwide. The innovative campaign turned the company into one of the best-known names in cyberspace—all because Brandt, now AOL's vice chair and chief marketing officer, guided by the principle of connecting consumers, put her resources into empowering AOL's target community rather than sinking time and money into slick advertising.

As AOL's experience illustrates, a strong strategic principle can inform high-level corporate decisions—those involving divestitures, for example—as well as decisions made by department heads or others further down in an organization. It also frees up CEOs from constant involvement in the implementation of their strategic mandates. "The genius of a great leader is to leave behind him a situation that common sense, without the grace of genius, can deal with successfully," said journalist and political thinker Walter Lippman. Scratch the surface of a number of high-performing companies, and you'll find that strategic principles are connecting the strategic insights—if not always the genius—of leaders with the pragmatic sense of line operators.

Now More Than Ever. In the past, a strategic principle was nice to have but was hardly required, unless a company found itself in a trying business situation. Today, many companies simultaneously face four situations that make a strategic principle crucial for success: decentralization, rapid growth, technological change, and institutional turmoil.

For the reasons mentioned above, *decentralization* is becoming common at companies of all stripes; thus, there is a corresponding need for a mechanism to ensure coherent strategic action. Especially in the case of diversified conglomerates, where strategy is formed in each of the business units, a strategic principle can help executives maintain consistency while giving unit managers the freedom to tailor their strategies to meet their own needs. It can also clarify the value of the center at such far-flung companies. For example, GE's long-standing strategic principle of always being number one or number two in an industry offers a powerful rationale for how a conglomerate can create value but still give individual units considerable strategic freedom.

A strategic principle is also crucial when a company is experiencing *rapid growth*. During such times, it's increasingly the case that lessexperienced managers are forced to make deci sions about nettlesome issues for which there may be no precedent. A clear and precise strategic principle can help counteract this shortage of experience. This is particularly true when a start-up company is growing rapidly in an established industry. For instance, as Southwest Airlines began to grow quickly, it might have been tempted to mimic its rivals' ultimately unsuccessful strategies if it hadn't had its own strategic principle to follow: "Meet customers' short-haul travel needs at fares competitive with the cost of automobile travel." Likewise, eBay, whose principle is "Focus on trading communities," might have been tempted, like many Internet marketplaces, to diversify into all sorts of services. But eBay has chosen to outsource certain services—for instance, management of the photos that sellers post on the site to illustrate the items they put up for bid—while it continues to invest in services like Billpoint, which lets sellers accept credit-card payments from bidders. EBay's strategic principle has ensured that the entire company stays focused on the core trading business.

The staggering pace of *technological change* over the past decade has been costly for companies that don't have a strategic principle. Never before in business has there been more uncertainty combined with so great an emphasis on speed. Managers in high-tech industries in particular must react immediately to sudden and unexpected developments. Often, the sum of the reactions across the organization ends up defining the company's strategic course. A strategic principle—for example, Dell's mandate to sell direct to end users—helps ensure that the decisions made by frontline managers in such circumstances add up to a consistent, coherent strategy.

Finally, a strategic principle can help provide continuity during periods of *organizational turmoil.* An increasingly common example of turmoil in this era of short-term CEOs is leadership succession. A new CEO can bring with him or her a new strategy—but not necessarily a new strategic principle. For instance, when Jack Brennan took over as chairman and CEO at Vanguard five years ago, the strategic transition was seamless, despite some tension around the leadership transition. He maintained the mutual fund company's strategic principle—"Unmatchable value for the investor- owner"—thereby allowing managers to pursue their strategic objectives without many of the distractions so often associated with leadership changes.

Strategic Principles in Action. Strategic principles and their benefits can best be understood by seeing the results they create.

Forcing Trade-Offs at Southwest Airlines. Southwest Airlines is one of the air-travel industry's great success stories. It is the only airline that hasn't lost money in the past 25 years. Its stock price rose a compounded 21,000% between 1972 and 1992, and it is up 300% over the past five years, which have been difficult ones in the airline industry. For most companies, such rapid growth would cause problems: legions of frontline employees taking up the mantle of decision making from core executives and, inevitably, stumbling. But in Southwest's case, employees have consistently made trade-offs in keeping with the company's strategic principle.

The process for making important and complicated decisions about things like network design, service offerings, route selection and pricing, cabin design, and ticketing procedures is straightforward. That's because the tradeoffs required by the strategic principle are clear. For instance, in 1983, Southwest initiated service to Denver, a potentially high-traffic destination and a seemingly sensible expansion of the company's presence in the Southwestern United States. However, the airline experienced longer and more consistent delays at Denver's Stapleton airport than it did anywhere else. These delays were caused not by slow turnaround at the gate but by increased taxi time on the runway and planes circling in the air because of bad weather. Southwest had to decide whether the potential growth from serving the Denver market was worth the higher costs associated with the delays, which would ultimately be reflected in higher ticket prices. The company turned to its strategic principle: would the airline be able to maintain fares competitive with the cost of automobile travel? Clearly, in Denver at least, it couldn't. Southwest pulled out of Stapleton three years after inaugurating the service there and has not returned.

Testing Action at AOL. A large part of AOL's ability to move so far and so fast across untrod ground lies in its practice of testing potential moves against its strategic principle. Employees who see attractive opportunities can ask themselves whether seizing one or several will lead to deeper consumer connectivity or broader distribution. Take, for example, line manager Katherine Borescnik, now president of programming at AOL. Several years ago she noticed increased activity—call it consumer connectivity—around the bulletinboard folders created on the site by two irreverent stock analysts and AOL subscribers. She offered the analysts the chance to create their own financial site, which became Motley Fool, a point of connection and information for do-it-yourself investors.

And AOL's strategic principle reaches even deeper into the organization. The hundreds of acquisitions and deals that AOL has made in the past few years have involved numerous employees. While top officers make final decisions, employees on the ground first screen opportunities against the company's strategic principle. Furthermore, the integration efforts following acquisitions, while choreographed at the top, are executed by a coterie of managers who ensure that the plans comply with the company's strategic principle. "We have succeeded, both in our deal making and in our integration, because our acquisitions have all been driven by our focus on how our customers communicate and connect," says Ken Novack, AOL Time Warner's vice chairman.

AOL's massive merger with Time Warner clearly furthers AOL's strategic principle of enabling consumer connections "anytime, anywhere" by adding TV and cable access to the Internet company's current dial-up access on the personal computer. But integrating this merger, which will involve hundreds of employees making and executing thousands of decisions, may be the ultimate test of AOL's strategic principle.

Experimenting Within Boundaries at Vanguard. The Vanguard Group, with $565 billion in assets under management, has quietly be come a giant in the mutual fund industry. The company's strategy is a response to the inability of most mutual funds to beat the market, often because of the cost of their marketing activities, overhead, and frequent transactions. To counter this, Vanguard discourages investors from making frequent trades and keeps its own overhead and advertising costs far below the industry average. It passes the savings directly to investors, who, because Vanguard is a mutual rather than a public company, are the fund's owners.

While this was Vanguard's founding strategy, for years the company didn't communicate it widely to employees. As a result, they often suggested initiatives that were out of sync with the company's core strategy. "Midlevel managers would walk in holding the newspaper saying, 'Look at what Fidelity just did. How about if we do that?'" Jack Brennan says. It wasn't apparent to them that Vanguard's strategy was very different from that of its rival, which has higher costs and isn't mutually owned. Over the years, Vanguard has invested considerable energy in crafting a strategic principle and using it to disseminate the company's strategy. Now, because employees understand the strategy, top management trusts them to initiate moves on their own.

Consider Vanguard's response to a major trend in retail fund distribution: the emergence of the on-line channel. Industry surveys indicated that most investors wanted Internet access to their accounts and that on-line traders were more active than off-line traders. So Vanguard chose to integrate the Internet into its service in a way that furthered its strategy of keeping costs low: basically, it lets customers access their accounts on-line, but it limits Web-based trading. It should be noted that the original ideas for Vanguard's on-line initiatives, including early ventures with AOL, were conceived by frontline employees, not senior executives.

Brennan says the company's strategic principle affects the entire management process, including hiring, training, performance measurement, and incentives. He points to a hidden benefit of having a strong strategic principle: "You're more efficient and can run with a leaner management team because everyone is on the same page."

Creating a Strategic Principle. Many of the best and most conspicuous examples of strategic principles come from companies that were founded on them, companies such as eBay, Dell, Vanguard, Southwest Airlines, and Wal-Mart ("Low prices, every day"). The founders of those companies espoused a clear guiding principle that summarized the essence of what would become a full-blown business strategy. They attracted investors who believed it, hired employees who bought into it, and targeted customers who wanted it.

Leaders of long-standing multinationals, like GE, crafted their strategic principles at a critical juncture: when increasing corporate complexity threatened to confuse priorities on the front line and obscure the essence that truly differentiated their strategy from that of their rivals.

Companies in this second category, which represents most of the companies that are likely to contemplate creating a strategic principle, face a demanding exercise. It probably comes as no surprise that identifying the essence of your strategy so it can be translated into a simple, memorable phrase is no easy task. It's a bit like corporate genomics: the principle must isolate and capture the corporate equivalent of the genetic code that differentiates your company from its competitors. This is somewhat like identifying the 2% of DNA that separates man from monkey—or, even more difficult and more apt, the .1% of DNA that differentiates each human being.

There are different ways to identify the elements that must be captured in a strategic principle, but keep in mind that a corporate strategy represents a plan to effectively allocate scarce resources to achieve sustainable competitive advantage. Managers need to ask themselves: how does my company allocate those resources to create value in a unique way, one that differentiates my company from competitors? Try to summarize the answer in a brief phrase that captures the essence of your company's point of differentiation.

Once that idea has been expressed in a phrase, test the strategic principle for its enduring nature. Does it capture what you intend to do for only the next three to five years, or does it capture a more timeless essence: the genetic code of your company's competitive differentiation? Then test the strategic principle for its communicative power. Is it clear, concise, and memorable? Would you feel proud to paint it on the side of a truck, as Wal-Mart does?

Finally, test the principle for its ability to promote and guide action. In particular, assess whether it exhibits the three attributes of an effective strategic principle. Will it force tradeoffs? Will it serve as a test for the wisdom of a particular business move, especially one that might promote short-term profits at the expense of long-term strategy? Does it set boundaries within which people will nonetheless be free to experiment?

Given the importance of getting your strategic principle right, it is wise to gather feedback on these questions from executives and other employees during an incubation period. Once you are satisfied that the statement is accurate and compelling, disseminate it throughout the organization.

Of course, just as a brilliant strategy is worthless unless it is implemented, a powerful strategic principle is of no use unless it is communicated effectively. When CEO Jack Welch talks about aligning employees around GE's strategy and values, he emphasizes the need for consistency, simplicity, and repetition. The approach is neither flashy nor complicated, but it takes enormous discipline and could scarcely be more important. Welch has so broadly evangelized GE's "Be number one or number two" strategic principle that employees are not the only ones to chant the rant. So can most business writers, MBA students, and managers at other companies.

When Rethinking Is Required No strategy is eternal, nor is any strategic principle. But even if the elements of your strategy change, the very essence of it is likely to remain the same. Thus, your strategy may shift substantially as your customers' demographics and needs change. It may have to be modified in light of your company's changing costs and assets compared with those of competitors. Strategic half-lives are shortening, and, in general, strategy should be reviewed every quarter and updated every year. But while it's worth revisiting your strategic principle every time you reexamine your strategy, it is likely to change only when there is a significant shift in the basic economics and opportunities of your market caused by, say, legislation or a completely new technology or business model.

It's All in a Phrase

A handful of companies have distilled their strategy into a phrase and have used it to drive consistent strategic action throughout their organizations.

Company	Strategic Principle
America Online	Consumer connectivity first— anytime, anywhere
Dell	Be direct
eBay	Focus on trading communities
General Electric	Be number one or number two in every industry in which we compete, or get out
Southwest Airlines	Meet customers' short-haul travel needs at fares competitive with the cost of automobile travel
Vanguard	Unmatchable value for the investor-owner
Wal-Mart	Low prices, every day

Even then, your strategic principle may need only refining or expanding. GE's strategic principle has been enhanced, but not replaced, since Welch articulated it in 1981. Similarly, AOL's strategic principle will need to be broadened, but not necessarily jettisoned, following its merger with Time Warner. Ultimately, the merged company's strategic principle will also need to embody the importance of high-quality and relevant content, Time Warner's hallmark.

Vanguard takes explicit steps to ensure that the direction provided by its strategic principle remains current. For example, as part of an internal "devil's advocacy" process, managers are divided into groups to critique and defend past decisions and current policies. Recently, the group reconsidered two major strategic policies: the prohibitions against opening branch offices and against acquiring money management firms. After considerable discussion, the policies remained in place. According to CEO Brennan, "Sometimes the greatest value [of revisiting our strategic principle] is reconfirming what we're already doing." At the same time, Vanguard has the process to identify when change is needed.

Fundamental Principles. Respondents to Bain's annual survey of executives on the usefulness of management tools repeatedly cite the key role a mission statement can play in a company's success. We agree that a mission statement is crucial for promulgating a company's values and building a robust corporate culture. But it still leaves a large gap in a company's management communications portfolio. At least as important as a mission statement is something that promulgates a company's strategy—that is, a strategic principle.

The ability of frontline employees to execute a company's strategy without close central oversight is vital as the pace of technological change accelerates and as companies grow rapidly and become increasingly decentralized. To drive such behavior, a company needs to give employees a mandate broad enough to encourage enterprising behavior but specific enough to align employees' initiatives with company strategy.

While not a perfect analogy, the U.S. Constitution is in some ways like a strategic principle. It articulates and embodies the essence of the country's "strategy" to guarantee liberty and justice for all of its citizens—while providing direction to those drafting the laws and regulations that implement the strategy. While no corporate strategy has liberty and justice at its heart, the elements of an effective strategy are just as central to the success of a company as those concepts are to the prosperity of the United States. And in neither case will success be realized unless the core strategy is communicated broadly and effectively.

The Idea in Brief

Southwest Airlines keeps soaring. Ist stock price rose a compounded 21,000% between 1972 and 1992 and leapt 300% between 1995 and 2000.

Why does Southwest succeed while so many other airlines fail? Because it sticks to its powerful strategic principle: "Meet customers' short-haul travel needs at fares competitive with the cost of automobile travel." This pithy, memorable, actionoriented phrase distills Southwest's unique strategy and communicates it throughout the company.

An effective strategic principle lets a company simultaneously:

- maintain strategic focus, • empower workers to innovate and take risks,
- seize fleeting opportunities,
- create products and services that meet subtle shifts in customers' needs.

In today's rapidly changing world, companies must integrate decentralized decision making *with* coherent, strategic action. A well-crafted, skillfully implemented strategic principle lets them strike that delicate balance.

HALLMARKS OF POWERFUL STRATEGIC PRINCIPLES

A successful strategic principle:

Forces trade-offs between competing resources.

Example: Southwest Airlines' 1983 expansion to the high-traffic Denver area *seemed* sensible. But unusually long delays there due to bad weather and taxi time would have forced Southwest to increase ticket prices preventing it from adhering to its strategic principle of offering air fares competitive with the cost of auto travel. The company pulled out of Denver.

Tests the strategic soundness of particular decisions by linking leaders' strategic insights with line operators' pragmatic sense.

Example: AOL's strategic principle,"Consumer connectivity first anytime, anywhere," tested the wisdom of a powerful business decision: expanding AOL's global network through alliances with local partners, rather than using its own technology everywhere. Partners' understanding of local culture greatly increased customers' connectivity.

Sets clear boundaries within which employees operate and experiment.

Example: At mutual-fund giant The Vanguard Group, frontline employees conceived a potent idea: Let customers access their accounts on-line, but limit on-line trading. This move kept Vanguard's costs low, enabling the company to stick to its strategic principle: creating "unmatchable value for investors/ owners."

CREATING AND COMMUNICATING YOUR STRATEGIC PRINCIPLE

Capturing and communicating the essence of your company's strategy in a simple, memorable, actionable phrase isn't easy. These steps can help:

Transforming Corner-Office Strategy into Frontline Action

1. Draft a working strategic principle. Summarize your *corporate strategy*—your plan to allocate scarce resources in order to create value that distinguishes you from competitors—in a brief phrase. That phrase becomes your working *strategic principle.*

2. Test its endurance. A good strategic principle endures. Ask: Does our working strategic principle capture the timeless essence of our company's unique competitive value?

3. Test its communicative power. Ask: Is the phrase clear, concise, memorable? Would you feel proud to paint it on the side of your firm's trucks, as Wal-Mart does?

4. Test its ability to promote and guide action. Ask: Does the principle exhibit the three essential attributes: forcing trade-offs, testing the wisdom of business moves, setting boundaries for employees' experimentation?

5. Communicate it. Communicate your strategic principle consistently, simply, and repeatedly. You'll know you've succeeded when employees—as well as business writers, MBA students, and competitors—all "chant the rant."

CHAPTER 6

Strategy as Revolution

Let's admit it. Corporations around the world are reaching the limits of incrementalism. Squeezing another penny out of costs, getting a product to market a few weeks earlier, responding to customers' inquiries a little bit faster, ratcheting quality up one more notch, capturing another point of market share – those are the obsessions of managers today. But pursuing incremental improvements while rivals reinvent the industry is like fiddling while Rome burns.

Look at any industry and you will see three kinds of companies. First are the rule makers, the incumbents that built the industry. IBM, CBS, United Airlines, Merrill Lynch, Sears, Coca-Cola, and the like are the creators and protectors of industrial orthodoxy. They are the oligarchy. Next are the rule takers, the companies that pay homage to the industrial "lords." Fujitsu, ABC, U.S. Air, Smith Barney, J.C. Penney, and numerous others are those peasants. Their life is hard. Imagine working at Fujitsu for 30 years trying to catch IBM in the mainframe business, or being McDonnell Douglas to Boeing, or Avis to Hertz. We Try Harder may be a great advertising slogan, but it's depressingly futile as a strategy. What good will it do to work harder to follow the rules when some com panies are rewriting them? IKEA, the Body Shop, Charles Schwab, Dell Computer, Swatch, Southwest Airlines, and many more are the rule breakers. Shackled neither by convention nor by respect for precedent, these companies are intent on overturning the industrial order. They are the malcontents, the radicals, the industry revolutionaries.

Never has the world been more hospitable to industry revolutionaries and more hostile to industry incumbents. The fortifications that protected the industrial oligarchy are crumbling under the weight of deregulation, technological upheaval, globalization, and social change. But it's not just the forces of change that are overturning old industrial structures – it's the actions of companies that harness those forces for the cause of revolution.

What if your company is more ruling class than revolutionary? You can either surrender the future to revolutionary challengers or revolutionize the way your company creates strategy. What is required is not a little tweak to the traditional planning process but a new philosophical foundation: strategy *is* revolution; everything else is tactics.

The following ten principles can help a company liberate its revolutionary spirit and dramatically increase its chances of discovering truly revolutionary strategies. Companies in industries as diverse as personal care products, information services, food processing, insurance, and telecommunications have internalized and acted on these principles. Every organization, however, must interpret and apply them in its own way. These are not a set of step-by-step instructions but a way of thinking about the challenge of creating strategy – the challenge of becoming an industry revolutionary.

Principle 1: Strategic planning isn't strategic. Consider your company's planning process. Which describes it best – column A, on the left, or column B, on the right?

Unless your company is truly exceptional, you've probably admitted that the words in column A are more fitting than those in column B. In the vast majority of companies, strategic planning is a calendar-driven ritual, not an exploration of the potential for revolution. The strategy-making process tends to be reductionist, based on simple rules and heuristics. It works from today forward, not from the future back, implicitly assuming, whatever the evidence to the contrary, that the future will be more or less like the present. Only a tiny percentage of an industry's conventions are ever challenged, rendering strategy making largely extrapolative. An industry's boundaries are taken as a given; thus the question is how to position products and services within those boundaries rather than how to invent new, uncontested competitive space. Further, the planning process is generally elitist, harnessing only a small proportion of an organization's creative potential.

Perhaps most disturbing, strategy making is often assumed to be easy, especially in comparison with implementing strategy. But of course strategy making is easy when the process limits the scope of discovery, the breadth of involvement, and the amount of intellectual effort expended. Of course the process is easy when its goal is something far short of revolution. How often has strategic planning produced true strategic innovation? No wonder that in many organizations, corporate planning departments are being disbanded. No wonder that consulting firms are doing less and less "strategy" work and more and more "implementation" work.

The essential problem in organizations today is a failure to distinguish *planning* from *strategizing*.1 Planning is about programming, not discovering. Planning is for technocrats, not dreamers. Giving planners responsibility for creating strategy is like asking a bricklayer to create Michelangelo's *Pietà*.

Most executives know a strategy when they see one. Wal-Mart has a clear strategy; so does Federal Express. But recognizing a strategy that already exists is not enough. Where do strategies come from? How are they created? Strategizing is not a rote procedure – it is a quest. Any company that believes that planning can yield strategy will find itself under the curse of incrementalism while freethinking newcomers lead successful insurrections.

Principle 2: Strategy making must be subversive. Galileo challenged the centrality of Earth and man in the cosmos. The American colonists challenged the feudal dependencies and inherited privileges of European society. Picasso and other modernists challenged representational art. Einstein challenged Newtonian physics. Revolutionaries are subversive, but their goal is not subversion. What the defenders of orthodoxy see as subversiveness, the champions of new thinking see as enlightenment.

If there is to be any hope of industry revolution, the creators of strategy must cast off industrial conventions. For instance, Anita Roddick, the founder of the Body Shop, turned Charles Revson's hope-in-a-bottle formula on its head. Instead of assuming, as the cosmetics industry always had, that women lack self-confidence and will pay inflated prices for simple formulations if they believe that they will make them more attractive, Roddick assumed that women have self-esteem and just want lighthearted, environmentally responsible products. Roddick wasn't kidding when she said, "I watch where the cosmetics industry is going and then walk in the opposite direction."

Identify the 10 or 20 most fundamental beliefs that incumbents in your industry share. What new opportunities present themselves when you relax those beliefs? Consider the hotel industry's definition of a day, which begins when you check in and ends at noon, when you must check out. But if you check in at 1 A.M. after a grueling journey, why should you have to check out at the same time or pay the same amount as the person who arrived at 5 the previous afternoon? If a rental-car company can manage a fleet of cars on a rotating 24-hour basis, why can't a hotel do exactly the same with a fleet of rooms?

Rule makers and rule takers are the industry. Rule breakers set out to redefine the industry, to invent the new by challenging the old. Ask yourself, What are the fundamental conventions we have examined and abandoned in our company? Can you think of more than one or two? Can you think of any at all? If not, why not? As a senior executive, are you willing to embrace a subversive strategymaking process?

Principle 3: The bottleneck is at the top of the bottle. In most companies, strategic orthodoxy has some very powerful defenders: senior managers. Imagine an organizational pyramid with senior managers at the apex. (It has become fashionable to draw the pyramid with customers at the top and senior managers at the bottom. But as long as senior managers retain their privileges – corporate aircraft, spacious suites, and so on – I prefer to leave the pointy end at the top.) Where are you likely to find people with the least diversity of experience, the largest investment in the past, and the greatest reverence for industrial dogma? At the top. And where will you find the people responsible for creating strategy? Again, at the top.

The organizational pyramid is a pyramid of experience. But experience is valuable only to the extent that the future is like the past. In industry after industry, the terrain is changing so fast that experience is becoming irrelevant and even dangerous. Unless the strategy-making process is freed from the tyranny of experience, there is little chance of industry revolution. If you're a senior executive, ask yourself these questions: Has a decade or two of experience made me more willing or less willing to challenge my industry's conventions? Have I become more curious or less curious about what is happening beyond the traditional boundaries of my industry? Be honest. As Ralph Waldo Emerson wrote, "There are always two parties, the party of the past and the party of the future; the establishment and the movement." To which party do you belong?

Principle 4: Revolutionaries exist in every company. It is often said that you cannot find a pro-change constituency in a successful company. I disagree. It is more accurate to say that in a successful company you are unlikely to find a pro-change constituency among the top dozen or so officers.

Make no mistake: there are revolutionaries in your company. If you go down and out into your organization—out into the ranks of much maligned middle managers, for instance – you will find people straining against the bit of industrial orthodoxy. All too often, however, there is no process that lets those revolutionaries be heard. Their voices are muffled by the layers of cautious bureaucrats who separate them from senior managers. They are isolated and impotent, disconnected from others who share their passions. So, like economic refugees seeking greater opportunity in new lands, industry revolutionaries often abandon their employers to find more imaginative sponsors.

No one doubts that Jack Welch of General Electric, Percy Barnevik of ABB Asea Brown Boveri, and Ray Smith of Bell Atlantic are pro-change leaders. But rather than celebrating the exceptions – the few truly transformational executives who populate every tome on leadership – isn't the greater challenge to help the pro-change constituency that exists in every company find ist voice? Sure, there are some radical corporate leaders out there. But weren't they always revolutionaries at heart? Why couldn't they have had a much greater impact on their companies earlier in their careers? Perhaps they, too, found it difficult to challenge the combined forces of precedence, position, and power. It would be sad to conclude that a company can fully exploit the emotional and intellectual energy of a revolutionary only if he or she succeeds in navigating the tortuous route to the top. How many revolutionaries will wait patiently for such a chance?

As a corporate leader, do you know where the revolutionaries are in your own organization? Have you given them a say in the strategy-making process? One thing is certain: if you don't let the revolutionaries challenge you from within, they will eventually challenge you from without in the marketplace.

Principle 5: Change is not the problem; engagement is. Senior executives assume two things about change that squelch revolutionary strategies. The first assumption is that "people" – that is, middle managers and all the rest – are against change. The second assumption follows from the first: only a hero-leader can force a timid and backward-looking organization into the future. All too often, change epics portray the chief executive dragging the organization kicking and screaming into the twenty-first century.Enough of top-management grandstanding. Humankind would not have accomplished what it has over the past millennium if it was ambivalent about change or if the responsibility for change was vested in the socially or politically elite.

Imagine that I coax a flatlander to the top of a snow-covered mountain. After strapping two well-waxed skis onto the flatlander's feet, I give the nervous and unprepared nonskier a mighty push. He or she goes screaming over a precipice; I'm booked for murder. One could well understand how the novice might not appreciate the "change" I sought to engineer. Now imagine that the nonskier takes lessons for a few days. The now fledgling skier may ascend the same mountain and, though full of caution, voluntarily point the skis downhill. What has changed? Even with a bit of training, skiing is not without risks. But in the second scenario, the skier has been given a modicum of control–an ability to influence speed and direction.

All too often, when senior managers talk about change, they are talking about fear-inducing change, which they plan to impose on unprepared and unsuspecting employees. All too often, *change* is simply a code word for something nasty: a wrenching restructuring or reorganization. This sort of change is not about opening up new opportunities but about paying for the past mistakes of corporate leaders.

The objective is not to get people to support change but to give them responsibility for engendering change, some control over their destiny. You must engage the revolutionaries, wherever they are in your company, in a dialogue about the future. Does your strategy-making process do this? Do you secretly believe that change is better served by a more compliant organization than by a more vociferous one? When senior managers engage their organization in a quest for revolutionary strategies, they are invariably surprised to find out just how big the pro-change constituency actually is.

Principle 6: Strategy making must be democratic. Despite years of imploring people to bring their brains to work, to get involved in quality circles, process reengineering, and the like, senior managers have seldom urged them to participate in the process of strategy creation. But if senior managers can't address the challenge of operational improvements by themselves – witness their reliance on quality circles, suggestion systems, and processimprovement task forces – why would they be able to take on the challenge of industry revolution? After all, what do a company's top 40 or 50 executives have to learn from one another? They've been talking at one another for years. Their positions are well rehearsed, and they can finish one another's sentences. In fact, there is often a kind of intellectual incest among the top officers of a large company.

The capacity to think creatively about strategy is distributed widely in an enterprise. It is impossible to predict exactly where a revolutionary idea is forming; thus the net must be cast wide. In many of the companies I work with, hundreds and sometimes thousands of people get involved in crafting strategy. They are asked to look deeply into potential discontinuities, help define and elaborate the company's core competencies, ferret out corporate orthodoxies, and search for unconventional strategic options. In one company, the idea for a multimillion-dollar opportunity came from a twenty-something secretary. In another company, some of the best ideas about the organization's core competencies came from a forklift operator.

To help revolutionary strategies emerge, senior managers must supplement the hierarchy of experience with a hierarchy of imagination. This can be done by dramatically extending the strategy franchise. Three constituencies that are usually underrepresented in the strategy-making process must have a disproportionate say. The first constituency is young people – or, more accurately, people with a youthful perspective. Of course, some 30-year-olds are "young fogies," but most young people live closer to the future than people with gray hair. It is ironic that the group with the biggest stake in the future is the most disenfranchised from the process of strategy creation.

Strategy as Revolution

My definition of success in a strategy-creation process is exemplified by an executive committee spending half a day learning something new from a 25-year-old. Recently, a young technical employee in an accounting company explained the implications of virtual reality to the senior partners. His pitch went like this: "Think about a complex set of corporate accounts. How easily and quickly can you uncover the subtle relationships among the numbers that might point to a problem or opportunity? Virtual reality will allow you to 'fly' over a topography of corporate accounts. That big black hole over there is a revenue shortfall, and that red mountain is unsold inventory. A few small companies are already working on applying virtual reality to financial accounts. Are we going to get on board or risk getting left behind?" The partners actually learned something new that day. When was the last time a Generation-X employee in your company exchanged ideas with the executive committee?

The people at an organization's geographic periphery are the second constituency that deserves a larger say in strategy making. The capacity for strategic innovation increases proportionately with each mile you move away from headquarters. For a U.S. company, the periphery might be India, Singapore, Brazil, or even the West Coast. For a Japanese company, it might be Indonesia or the United States. At the periphery of an organization, people are forced to be more creative because they usually have fewer resources, and they are exposed to ideas and developments that do not conform to the company's orthodoxies. Remember the old Chinese defense of local exceptions to central rule: The emperor is far away and the hills are high. But again, in many companies the periphery has little say in the strategy-making process. If a company aims to generate 40% or 50% of its revenues in international markets, international voices should have a say in the strategymaking process to match.

The third constituency that deserves a disproportionate say is newcomers, people who have not yet been co-opted by an industry's dogma. Perhaps you've looked outside your company or industry for senior executives with fresh perspectives. But how systematically have you sought the advice of newcomers at all levels who have not yet succumbed to the dead hand of orthodoxy? Think about last year's strategic-planning process. How many new voices were heard? How hard did you work to create the opportunity to be surprised?

Inviting new voices into the strategy-making process, however, is not enough. Senior executives must ensure that they don't drown out people who are overly inclined to deference. In one company, the young representative of a strategycreation team presented the group's findings to the management committee. When the anxious young employee showed up at the appointed place and hour, he was confronted by a daunting spectacle: 12 executives, most with more than 20 years of seniority, ensconced in high-backed leather chairs arranged around an enormous boardroom table. The brave young manager never stood a chance. Less than five minutes into the four-hour talk, he was being pelted with disbelief and skepticism. The management committee demonstrated its capacity for (unwitting) intimidation and learned little.

After this fiasco, the people attempting to facilitate the dialogue saw to it that the setting for the next meeting was very different. First, it was held off-site on neutral territory. Second, all 25 members of the strategy-creation team were invited; thus they outnumbered the executives. Third, the management committee sat in ordinary chairs arranged in a semicircle – they had no table behind which to hide. Finally, the management committee was asked to hold all comments during the presentation. Afterward, each member of the management committee was assigned two members of the team for a four-hour discussion that focused on how the team had arrived at its conclusions. The next morning, the executives were willing to admit that they had learned a lot, and they were able to give helpful advice to the team members about where they should deepen and expand their work.

Strategy as Revolution

That is strategy making as a democratic process. People should have a say in their destiny, a chance to influence the direction of the enterprise to which they devote their energy. The idea of democracy has become so enervated, and the individual's sense of responsibility to the community so feeble, that they can both be summarized in the slogan One Person, One Vote. That notion represents not the full ideal of democracy but its minimal precondition. If one exercises the rights of citizenship only once every 1,461 days, can one claim to be a citizen in any meaningful sense? In the corporate sphere, suggestion schemes and town hall meetings are but the tender shoots of a pluralistic process. Democracy is not simply about the right to be heard; it is about the opportunity to influence opinion and action. It is about being impatient and impassioned, informed and involved. The real power of democracy is that not only the elite can shape the agenda. One's voice can be bigger than one's vote. Susan B. Anthony, Martin Luther King, Jr., Ralph Nader, Rush Limbaugh, and Jesse Jackson have all had an influence on political thought and action that has gone far beyond a single vote.

What percentage of the employees in your company have ever seen a copy of the corporate strategy, much less participated in its creation? No wonder that what passes for strategy is usually sterile and uninspiring. Saul Alinsky, one of the most effective social revolutionaries in the United States this century, wrote this about the output of top-down, elitist planning: "It is not a democratic program but a monumental testament to lack of faith in the ability and intelligence of the masses of people to think their way through to the successful solution of their problems.... the people will have little to do with it." That which is imposed is seldom embraced. An elitist approach to strategy creation engenders little more than compliance.

Principle 7: Anyone can be a strategy activist. Perhaps senior managers are reluctant to give up their monopoly on the creation of strategy. After all, how often has the monarch led the uprising? What can so-called ordinary employees do to ensure that their company becomes or remains the author of industry revolution? Plenty. They can become strategy activists. Today frontline employees and middle managers are inclined to regard themselves more as victims than as activists. They have lost confidence in their ability to shape the future of their organizations. They have forgotten that from Gandhi to Mandela, from the American patriots to the Polish shipbuilders, the makers of revolutions have not come from the top. Notwithstanding all the somber incantations that change must start at the top, is it realistic to expect that, in any reasonable percentage of cases, senior managers will start an industry revolution? No.

In one large company, a small group of middle managers who were convinced that their company was in danger of forfeiting the future to less conventional rivals established what they called a "delta team." The managers, none of whom was a corporate officer, had no mandate to change the company and asked no one for permission to do so. Over several months, they worked quietly and persistently to convince their peers that it was time to rethink the company's basic beliefs. This conviction gradually took root among a cross section of managers, who started asking senior executives difficult questions about whether the company was actually in control of its destiny. Did the company have a unique and compelling view of its future? Was the company ahead of or behind the industry's change curve? Was it at the center or on the periphery of the coalitions that were reshaping the industry? Ultimately, senior managers conceded that they could not answer those questions. The result was a concerted effort, spanning several months and hundreds of employees, to find opportunities to create industry revolution. Out of this effort came a fundamental change in the company's concept of its mission, a score of new and unconventional business opportunities, and a doubling of revenues over the next five years.

Activists are not anarchists. Their goal is not to tear down but to reform. They know that an uninvolved citizenry deserves whatever fate befalls it, as do cautious and cringing middle managers. People who care about their country– or their organization – don't wait for permission to act. Activists don't shape their opinions to fit the prejudices of those they serve. They are patriots intent on protecting the enterprise from mediocrity, self-interest, and mindless veneration of the past. Not every activist ends up a hero. Shortly after he became president of the Supreme Soviet, Nikita Khrushchev gave a speech to a large group of Communist Party leaders in which he denounced the excesses of Stalin. During a pause, a voice rang out from the back of the hall, "You were there. Why didn't you stop him?" Taken aback by such impertinence, Khrushchev thundered, "Who said that?" The questioner slunk low in his seat and was silent. After a long, uncomfortable minute in which his eyes raked the audience, Khrushchev replied, "Now you know why." It is often safer to be silent. The corporate equivalent of Lubyanka is an office without a telephone or a window. Dissenters aren't shot for treason; they're asked to take a "lateral career move."

Listen to Thomas Paine: "Let them call me rebel and welcome, I feel no concern from it; but I should suffer the misery of devils, were I to make a whore of my soul." In a corporate context, this sounds like hyperbole. But think of the great companies that have fallen hopelessly behind the change curve because middle managers and first-level employees lacked the courage to speak up. To be an activist, one must care more for one's community than for one's position in the hierarchy. The goal is not to leave senior executives behind. The goal is not to stage a palace coup. But when senior managers are distracted, when planning has supplanted strategizing, and when more energy is being devoted to protecting the past than to creating the future, activists must step forward.

Principle 8: Perspective is worth 50 IQ points.2Without enlightenment, there can be no revolution. To discover opportunities for industry revolution, one must look at the world in a new way, through a new lens. It is impossible to make people smarter, but you can help them see with new eyes. Remember when you took your first economics course? I do. It didn't make me any smarter, but it gave me a new lens through which to look at the world. Much that had been invisible – the link between savings and investment, between interest rates and exchange rates, and between supply and demand—suddenly became visible.

A view of the corporation as a bundle of core competencies rather than a collection of business units is a new perspective. A view of discontinuities as levers for change rather than threats to the status quo is a new perspective. A view that imagination   rather than investment determines an organization's capacity to be strategic is a new perspective.

Any company intent on creating industry revolution has four tasks. First, the company must identify the unshakable beliefs that cut across the industry – the industry's conventions. Second, the company must search for discontinuities in technology, lifestyles, working habits, or geopolitics that might create opportunities to rewrite the industry's rules. Third, the company must achieve a deep understanding of its core competencies. Fourth, the company must use all this knowledge to identify the revolutionary ideas, the unconventional strategic options, that could be put to work in its competitive domain. What one sees from the mountaintop is quite different from what one sees from the plain. There can be no innovation in the creation of strategy without a change in perspective.

Principle 9: Top-down and bottom-up are not the alternatives. The creation of strategy is usually characterized as either a topdown or bottom-up process. Strategy either emerges as a grand design at the top – think of Jack Welch's famous "three circles," which defined GE's future business focus—or bubbles up from lone entrepreneurs, such as the man who invented Post-It Notes at 3M. But all too often, top-down strategies are dirigiste rather than visionary. And in all too many companies, the entrepreneurial spark is more likely to be doused by a flood of corporate orthodoxy than fanned by resources and the support of senior executives. In my experience, new-venture divisions, skunk works, and the musings of research fellows are no more likely to engender an industry revolution than is an annual planning process.

Just as a political activist who fails to influence those with legislative authority will make little lasting difference, a strategy activist who fails to win senior managers' confidence will achieve nothing. Senior managers may not have a monopoly on imagination, but they do have a board-sanctioned monopoly on the allocation of resources. To bankroll the revolution, senior executives must believe, both intellectually and emotionally, in its aims. So although the revolution doesn't need to start at the top, it must ultimately be understood and endorsed by the top. In the traditional model of strategy creation, the thinkers are assumed to be at the top and the doers down below. In reality, the thinkers often lie deep in the organization, and senior managers simply control the means of doing.

To achieve diversity of perspective and unity of purpose, the strategy-making process must involve a deep diagonal slice of the organization. A top-down process often achieves unity of purpose: the few who are involved come to share a conviction about the appropriate course of action and can secure some degree of compliance from those below. A bottom-up process can achieve diversity of perspective: many voices are heard and many options are explored. But unity without diversity leads to dogma, and diversity without unity results in competing strategy agendas and the fragmentation of resources. Only a strategy-making process that is deep and wide can achieve both diversity and unity.

Bringing the top and bottom together in the creation of strategy will help bypass the usually painful and laborious process whereby a lowly employee champions an idea up the chain of command. Managers, many of whom may be more intent on protecting their reputations for prudence than on joining the ranks of the lunatic fringe, are likely to shoot down any revolutionary idea that reaches them. There are many ways of linking those on the bottom with those in the officer corps. Senior executives can sponsor a process of deep thinking about discontinuities, core competencies, and new rules that involves a cross section of the organization. Senior managers can participate as team members—together with secretaries, salespeople, and first-level engineers – in the search for revolutionary opportunities. An executive committee can devote one week per month to keeping up to speed with the revolutionary ideas that are gestating deep in the organization.

What senior executives must not do is ask a small, elite group or the "substitute brains" of a traditional strategyconsulting firm to go away and plot the company's future. With neither senior managers nor a substantial cross section of the organization involved, the output will likely be considered a bastard by all except those who created it.

Of course, senior managers must ultimately make hard choices about which revolutionary strategies to support and what resources to commit, but they must avoid the temptation to judge prematurely. In the quest for revolutionary strategies, a senior executive must be more student than magistrate. In one company, the CEO believed that the strategy-making team was responsible for convincing him that it had come up with the right answers. That is the wrong attitude. It is the CEO's responsibility to stay close enough to the organization's learning process that he or she can share employees' insights and understand their emerging convictions. In the traditional planning process, outcomes are likely to cluster closely around senior managers' prejudices; the gap between recommendations and preexisting predilections is likely to be low. But that is not the case in a more open-ended process of strategic discovery. If the goal is to ensure that the resource holders and the revolutionaries end up at the same place at the same time, senior executives must engage in a learning process alongside those at the vanguard of industry revolution.

Principle 10: You can't see the end from the beginning. A strategymaking process that involves a broad cross section of the company, delves deeply into discontinuities and competencies, and encourages employees to escape an industry's conventions will almost inevitably reach surprising conclusions. At EDS, such a process convinced many in the organization that it was not enough to be a business-to-business company. As the dividing line between professional life and personal life was blurring, EDS realized that it had to become capable of serving individuals as well as businesses. After an open and creative strategy-making process, EDS installed automated teller machines in many 7-Eleven stores. Months earlier, few would have anticipated, much less credited, such a move.

Not everyone enjoys surprises. Senior managers cannot predict where an open-ended strategy-making process will lead, but they cannot go only part of the way to industry revolution. If nervous executives open up a dialogue and then ignore the outcome, they will poison the well. In one company, senior managers articulated their reluctance to staff a strategy-making team with a cohort of young, out-of-the-box employees. The CEO was convinced that he needed to set clear boundaries on the work of the eager revolutionaries. Defending his desire to impose prior restraint on the strategy-creation process, he asked, "What if the team comes back with dumb ideas?" The response: "If that is the case, you have a bigger problem—dumb managers." Senior managers should be less worried about getting off-the-wall suggestions and more concerned about failing to unearth the ideas that will allow their company to escape the curse of incrementalism.

Though it is impossible to see the end from the beginning, an open-ended and inclusive process of strategy creation substantially lessens the challenge of implementation. Implementation is often more difficult than it need be because only a handful of people have been involved in the creation of strategy and only a few key executives share a conviction about the way forward. Too often, the planning process ends with the challenge of getting "buy-in," of getting what is in the heads of the bosses into the heads of the worker bees. But when several hundred employees share the task of identifying and synthesizing a set of unconventional strategic options, the conclusions take on an air of inevitability. In such a process, senior managers' task is less to "sell" the strategy than to ensure that the organization acts on the convictions that emerge. How often does the planning process start with senior executives asking what the rest of the organization can teach them about the future? Not often enough.

To invite new voices into the strategy-making process, to encourage new perspectives, to start new conversations that span organizational boundaries, and then to help synthesize unconventional options into a point of view about corporate direction —those are the challenges for senior executives who believe that strategy must be revolution.

Nine Routes to Industry Revolution. Unless you are an industry leader with an unassailable position – a status that, given the lessons of history, not even Microsoft would be wise to claim – you probably have a greater stake in staging a revolution than in preserving the status quo. The opportunities for revolution are many and mostly unexplored. How should a would-be revolutionary begin? By looking for ways to redefine products and services, market space, and even the entire structure of an industry.

Reconceiving a Product or Service

1. Radically Improving the Value Equation. In every industry, there is a ratio that relates price to performance: X units of cash buy Y units of value. The challenge is to improve that value ratio and to do so radically – 500% or 1,000%, not 10% or 20%. Such a fundamental redefinition of the value equation forces a reconception of the product or service.

Fidelity Investments, for instance, wondered why a person couldn't invest in foreign equity markets for tens or hundreds of dollars rather than thousands. On a recent flight, I heard one flight attendant say to another, "I just moved some of my investments from the Europe Fund to the Pacific Basin Fund." Such a comment would have been inconceivable a decade or two ago, but Fidelity and other mutual-fund revolutionaries have redefined the industry's value equation. Hewlett-Packard's printer business and IKEA are other value revolutionaries.

2. Separating Function and Form. Another way to challenge the existing concept of a product or service is to separate core benefits (function) from the ways in which those benefits are currently embodied in a product or service (form). Any organization that is able to distinguish form from function and then reconceive one or both has the opportunity to create an industry revolution.

Consider credit cards, which perform two functions. First, a credit card inspires a merchant to trust that you are who the card says you are: your name is embossed on the front, your signature appears on the back, and your photo may even appear in the corner. Nevertheless, credit card fraud is a rapidly escalating problem. In what form will "trust" be delivered in the future? Probably through biometric data: a handprint, voiceprint, or retinal scan. Any credit card maker that is not investing in those technologies today may be surprised by interlopers. Second, a credit card gives you permission to charge up to your credit limit. What new opportunities appear if you distinguish permission as a general function from the particular case of permission to charge? In many hotels, a card with a magnetic stripe gives guests "permission" to enter their rooms. Did credit card makers see the opportunity to use the cards in this way? No, the card security market is owned largely by newcomers.

3. Achieving Joy of Use. We live in a world that takes ease of use for granted. The new goal is joy of use. We want our products and services to be whimsical, tactile, informative, and just plain fun. Any company that can wrap those attributes around a mundane product or service has the chance to be an industry revolutionary.

What's the most profitable food retailer per square foot in the United States? Probably Trader Joe's, a cross between a gourmet deli and a discount warehouse, which its CEO, John Shields, calls a "fashion food retailer." Essentially without competition, its 74 stores were averaging annual sales of $1,000 per square foot in 1995 – twice the rate of conventional supermarkets and more than three times that of most specialty food shops. Customers shop Trader Joe's as much for entertainment as for sustenance. The store stocks dozens of offbeat foods – jasmine fried rice, salmon burgers, and raspberry salsa – as well as carefully selected, competitively priced staples. By turning shopping from a chore into a culinary treasure hunt, Trader Joe's has more than doubled its sales over the last five years to $605 million.

Redefining Market Space

4. Pushing the Bounds of Universality. Every company has an implicit notion of its served market: the types of individuals and institutions that are – and are not – customers. Revolutionary companies, however, focus not just on their served market but on the total imaginable market.

A few years back, who would have considered children a likely market for 35-millimeter film? Would you have given your $500 Nikon to an eight-year-old? Probably not. Parents today, however, think nothing of giving a disposable camera to a child for a day at the beach, a birthday party, or the family's vacation. The single-use camera has made access to photography virtually universal. In 1995, the single-use-camera market reached 50 million units, worth close to $1 billion at retail. From class to mass, adult to child, profes sional to consumer, and national to global, the traditional boundaries of market space are being redefined by revolutionary companies.

5. Striving for Individuality. No one wants to be part of a mass market. We'll all buy the same things – but only if we have to. Deep in our need to be ourselves, to be unique, are the seeds of industry revolution.

A woman who wants a perfect-fitting pair of jeans, for example, can now get measured at one of Levi Strauss's Personal Pair outlets, and a computer will pick out exactly the right size. The woman's specifications are sent to Levi's by computer, and her made-to order jeans arrive a few days later. The price? Just about $10 more than an off-the-shelf pair. Levi's plans to introduce the Personal Pair system to nearly 200 stores in the United States by the end of the decade. The company is counting on its revolutionary approach to put a considerable dent in the growing market for private-label jeans.

6. Increasing Accessibility. Most market spaces have temporal and geographic bounds: customers must go to a specific store at a specific location between certain hours. But market space is becoming cyberspace, and every day industry revolutionaries are resetting consumers' expectations about accessibility.

Consider First Direct, a bank that can be reached only by telephone. The fastest-growing bank in Great Britain, First Direct was opening 10,000 new accounts per month in mid-1995–the equivalent of two or three branches. The professionals and workaholics who make up First Direct's half million customers carry, on average, a balance that's ten times higher than the average balance at Midland Bank, First Direct's parent, while overall costs per client are 61% less. One of the first U.S. banks to experiment with so-called direct banking estimates that it will ultimately be able to close at least half of its branches.

Redrawing Industry Boundaries

7. Rescaling Industries. As industry revolutionaries seek out and exploit new national and global economies of scale, industries around the world–even office cleaning and haircutting – are consolidating at a fearsome pace. Any industry that was local, such as consumer banking, is becoming national. Any industry that was national, such as the airline business, is becoming global.

Every minute and a half, Service Corporation International buries or cremates someone, somewhere in the world. Performing 320,000 funerals per year, SCI has become the world's largest funeral operator in an industry that traditionally has been very fragmented. Most funeral operators have been family businesses. By buying up small operators, SCI has reaped economies of scale in purchasing, capital utilization (sharing hearses among operators, for example), marketing, and administration.

Of course, an industry can be scaled down as well as up. Bed-and-breakfast inns, microbreweries, local bakeries, and specialty retailers are the result of industries that have scaled down to serve narrow or local customer segments more effectively.

8. Compressing the Supply Chain. The cognoscenti use the word *disintermediation* in its literal sense: the removal of intermediaries. Wal-Mart, for instance, essentially turned the warehouse into a store, thus disintermediating the traditional small-scale retailer. And Xerox hopes to reinvent the way companies distribute printed documents by disintermediating trucking companies from the printing business. Why, Xerox asks, should annual reports, user manuals, catalogs, employee handbooks, and other printed matter be hauled across the country in trucks? Why not send the information digitally and print it close to where it is needed? Xerox is working with a variety of partners to stage this revolution.

9. Driving Convergence. Revolutionaries not only radically change the value-added structure within industries but also blur the boundaries between industries. Deregulation, the ubiquity of information, and new customer demands give revolutionaries the chance to transcend an industry's boundaries.

For example, a consumer can now get a credit card from General Motors, a mortgage from Prudential or GE Capital, a retirement account at Fidelity Investments, and a checkbook from Charles Schwab. Innovative hospitals "capitate" lives, guaranteeing to provide an individual with a full range of health services for a fixed sum per year. Insurance companies, such as Aetna, respond by refashioning themselves into health care providers. Boston Market offers hot family-style meals for takeout, and supermarkets respond by offering an ever wider selection of prepared foods, further blurring the boundary between the grocery and fastfood industries.

Industry revolutionaries don't ask what industry they are in. They know that an industry's boundaries today are about as meaningful as borders in the Balkans.

CHAPTER 7

Using the Balanced Scorecard as a Strategic Management System

As companies around the world transform themselves for competition that is based on information, their ability to exploit intangible assets has become far more decisive than their ability to invest in and manage physical assets. Several years ago, in recognition of this change, we introduced a concept we called the balanced scorecard. The balanced scorecard supplemented traditional financial measures with criteria that measured performance from three additional perspectives—those of customers, internal business processes, and learning and growth. It therefore enabled companies to track financial results while simultaneously monitoring progress in building the capabilities and acquiring the intangible assets they would need for future growth. The scorecard wasn't a replacement for financial measures; it was their complement.

Recently, we have seen some companies move beyond our early vision for the scorecard to discover its value as the cornerstone of a new strategic management system. Used this way, the scorecard addresses a serious deficiency in traditional management systems: their inability to link a company's long-term strategy with its short-term actions.

Most companies' operational and management control systems are built around financial measures and targets, which bear little relation to the company's progress in achieving long-term strategic objectives. Thus the emphasis most companies place on short-term financial measures leaves a gap between the development of a strategy and its implementation.

Managing Strategy: Four Processes

Managers using the balanced scorecard do not have to rely on short-term financial measures as the sole indicators of the company's performance. The scorecard lets them introduce four new management processes that, separately and in combination, contribute to linking long-term strategic objectives with short-term actions.

The first new process—translating the vision—helps managers build a consensus around the organization's vision and strategy. Despite the best intentions of those at the top, lofty statements about becoming "best in class," "the number one supplier," or an "empowered organization" don't translate easily into operational terms that provide useful guides to action at the local level. For people to act on the words in vision and strategy statements, those statements must be expressed as an integrated set of objectives and measures, agreed upon by all senior executives, that describe the long-term drivers of success.

The second process—communicating and linking—lets managers communicate their strategy up and down the organization and link it to departmental and individual objectives. Traditionally, departments are evaluated by their financial performance, and individual incentives are tied to short-term financial goals. The scorecard gives managers a way of ensuring that all levels of the organization understand the long-term strategy and that both departmental and individual objectives are aligned with it.

The third process—business planning—enables companies to integrate their business and financial plans. Almost all organizations today are implementing a variety of change programs, each with its own champions, gurus, and consultants, and each competing for senior executives' time, energy, and resources. Managers find it difficult to integrate those diverse initiatives to achieve their strategic goals—a situation that leads to frequent disappointments with the programs' results. But when managers use the ambitious goals set for balanced scorecard measures as the basis for allocating resources and setting priorities, they can undertake and coordinate only those initiatives that move them toward their longterm strategic objectives.

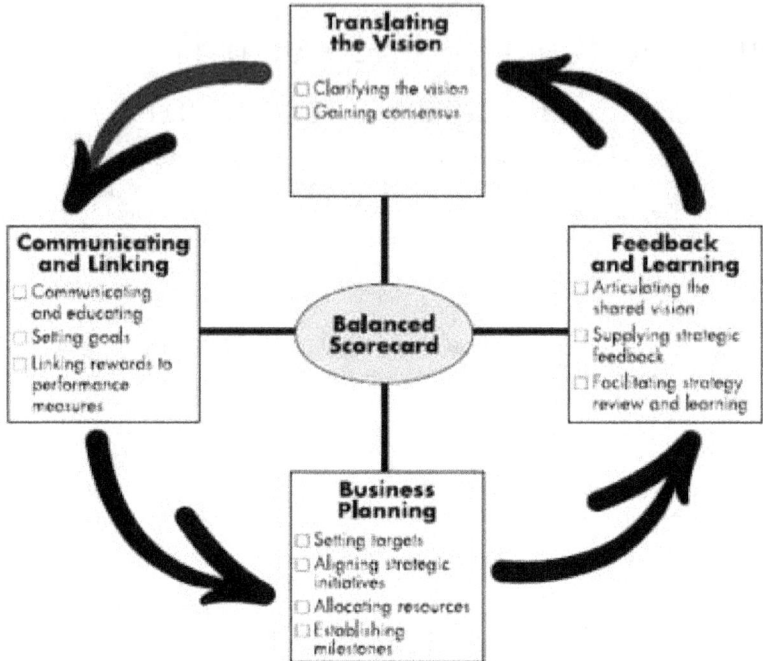

The fourth process—feedback and learning—gives companies the capacity for what we call strategic learning. Existing feedback and review processes focus on whether the company, its departments, or its individual employees have met their budgeted financial goals. With the balanced scorecard at the center of its management systems, a company can monitor short-term results from the three additional perspectives—customers, internal business processes, and learning and growth—and evaluate strategy in the light of recent performance. The scorecard thus enables companies to modify strategies to reflect real-time learning.

None of the more than 100 organizations that we have studied or with which we have worked implemented their first balanced scorecard with the intention of developing a new strategic management system. But in each one, the senior executives discovered that the scorecard supplied a framework and thus a focus for many critical management processes: departmental and individual goal setting, business planning, capital allocations, strategic initiatives, and feedback and learning. Previously, those processes were uncoordinated and often directed at short-term operational goals. By building the scorecard, the senior executives started a process of change that has gone well beyond the original idea of simply broadening the company's performance measures.

For example, one insurance company—let's call it National Insurance—developed its first balanced scorecard to create a new vision for itself as an underwriting specialist. But once National started to use it, the scorecard allowed the CEO and the senior management team not only to introduce a new strategy for the organization but also to overhaul the company's management system. The CEO subsequently told employees in a letter addressed to the whole organization that National would thenceforth use the balanced scorecard and the philosophy that it represented to manage the business.

Using the Balanced Scorecard as a Strategic Management System

National built its new strategic management system step-by-step over 30 months, with each step representing an incremental improvement. The iterative sequence of actions enabled the company to reconsider each of the four new management processes two or three times before the system stabilized and became an established part of National's overall management system. Thus the CEO was able to transform the company so that everyone could focus on achieving long-term strategic objectives—something that no purely financial framework could do.

Translating the Vision. The CEO of an engineering construction company, after working with his senior management team for several months to develop a mission statement, got a phone call from a project manager in the field. "I want you to know," the distraught manager said, "that I believe in the mission statement. I want to act in accordance with the mission statement. I'm here with my customer. What am I supposed to do?"

Translating Vision and Strategy: Four Perspectives

The mission statement, like those of many other organizations, had declared an intention to "use high-quality employees to provide services that surpass customers' needs." But the project manager in the field with his employees and his customer did not know how to translate those words into the appropriate actions. The phone call convinced the CEO that a large gap existed between the mission statement and employees' knowledge of how their day-to-day actions could contribute to realizing the company's vision.

Metro Bank (not its real name), the result of a merger of two competitors, encountered a similar gap while building its balanced scorecard. The senior executive group thought it had reached agreement on the new organization's overall strategy: "to provide superior service to targeted customers." Research had revealed five basic market segments among existing and potential customers, each with different needs. While formulating the measures for the customer-perspective portion became apparent that although the 25 senior executives agreed on the words of the strategy, each one had a different definition of superior service and a different image of the targeted customers.

The exercise of developing operational measures for the four perspectives on the bank's scorecard forced the 25 executives to clarify the meaning of the strategy statement. Ultimately, they agreed to stimulate revenue growth through new products and services and also agreed on the three most desirable customer segments. They developed scorecard measures for the specific products and services that should be delivered to customers in the targeted segments as well as for the relationship the bank should build with customers in each segment.

The scorecard also highlighted gaps in employees' skills and in information systems that the bank would have to close in order to deliver the selected value propositions to the targeted customers. Thus, creating a balanced scorecard forced the bank's senior managers to arrive at a consensus and then to translate their vision into terms that had meaning to the people who would realize the vision.

How One Company Built a Strategic Management System.

Communicating and Linking. "The top ten people in the business now understand the strategy better than ever before. It's too bad," a senior executive of a major oil company complained, "that we can't put this in a bottle so that everyone could share it." With the balanced scorecard, he can.

One company we have worked with deliberately involved three layers of management in the creation of its balanced scorecard. The senior executive group formulated the financial and customer objectives. It then mobilized the talent and information in the next two levels of managers by having them formulate the internal-business-process and learning-and-growth objectives that would drive the achievement of the financial and customer goals. For example, knowing the importance of satisfying customers' expectations of on-time delivery, the broader group identified several internal business processes—such as order processing, scheduling, and fulfillment—in which the company had to excel. To do so, the company would have to retrain frontline employees and improve the information systems available to them. The group developed performance measures for those critical processes and for staff and systems capabilities.

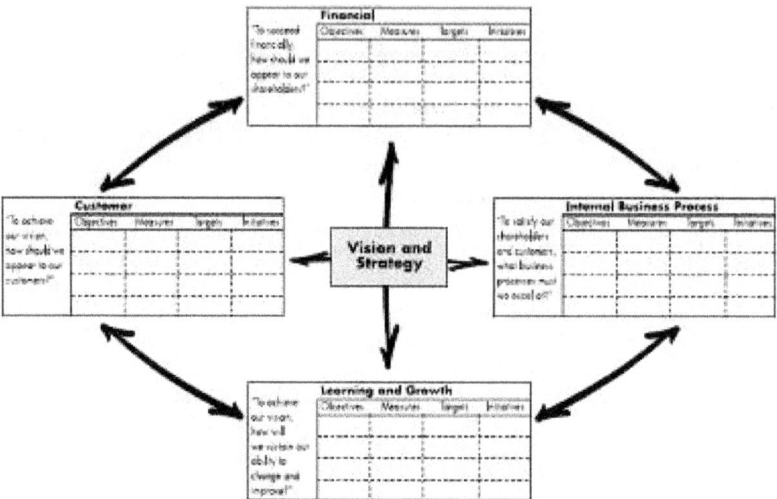

Broad participation in creating a scorecard takes longer, but it offers several advantages: Information from a larger number of managers is incorporated into the internal objectives; the managers gain a better understanding of the company's long-term strategic goals; and such broad participation builds a stronger commitment to achieving those goals. But getting managers to buy into the scorecard is only a first step in linking individual actions to corporate goals.

The balanced scorecard signals to everyone what the organization is trying to achieve for shareholders and customers alike. But to align employees' individual performances with the overall strategy, scorecard users generally engage in three activities: communicating and educating, setting goals, and linking rewards to performance measures.

Communicating and educating. Implementing a strategy begins with educating those who have to execute it. Whereas some organizations opt to hold their strategy close to the vest, most believe that they should disseminate it from top to bottom. A broad-based communication program shares with all employees the strategy and the critical objectives they have to meet if the strategy is to succeed. Onetime events such as the distribution of brochures or newsletters and the holding of "town meetings" might kick off the program. Some organizations post bulletin boards that illustrate and explain the balanced scorecard measures, then update them with monthly results. Others use groupware and electronic bulletin boards to distribute the scorecard to the desktops of all employees and to encourage dialogue about the measures. The same media allow employees to make suggestions for achieving or exceeding the targets.

The balanced scorecard, as the embodiment of business unit strategy, should also be communicated upward in the organization—to corporate headquarters and to the corporate board of directors. With the scorecard, business units can quantify and communicate their long-term strategies to senior executives using a comprehensive set of linked financial and nonfinancial measures. Such communication informs the executives and the board in specific terms that long-term strategies designed for competitive success are in place. The measures also provide the basis for feedback and accountability. Meeting short-term financial targets should not constitute satisfactory performance when other measures indicate that the long-term strategy is either not working or not being implemented well.

Should the balanced scorecard be communicated beyond the boardroom to external shareholders? We believe that as senior executives gain confidence in the ability of the scorecard measures to monitor strategic performance and predict future financial performance, they will find ways to inform outside investors about those measures without disclosing competitively sensitive information.

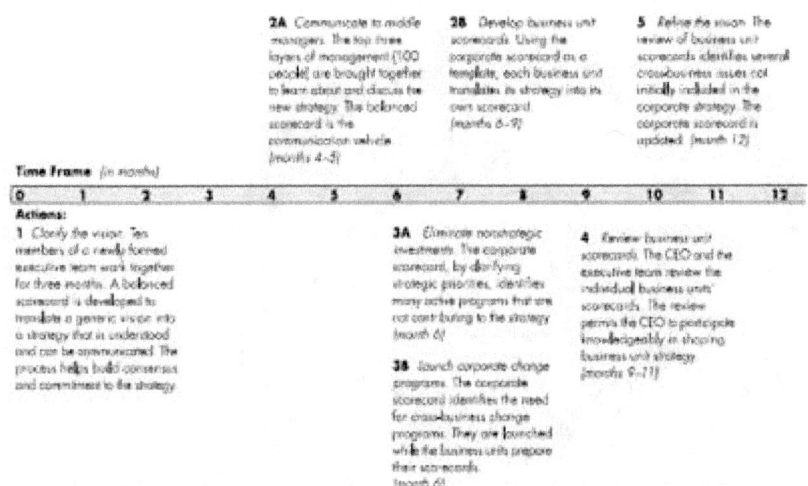

Skandia, an insurance and financial services company based in Sweden, issues a supplement to its annual report called "The Business Navigator"—"an instrument to help us navigate into the future and thereby stimulate renewal and development." The supplement describes Skandia's strategy and the strategic measures the company uses to communicate and evaluate the strategy. It also provides a report on the company's performance along those measures during the year. The measures are customized for each operating unit and include, for example, market share, customer satisfaction and retention, employee competence, employee empowerment, and technology deployment.

Communicating the balanced scorecard promotes commitment and accountability to the business's long-term strategy. As one executive at Metro Bank declared, "The balanced scorecard is both motivating and obligating."

Around the Balanced Scorecard. Setting goals. Mere awareness of corporate goals, however, is not enough to change many people's behavior. Somehow, the organization's high-level strategic objectives and measures must be translated into objectives and measures for operating units and individuals.

The exploration group of a large oil company developed a technique to enable and encourage individuals to set goals for themselves that were consistent with the organization's. It created a small, fold-up, personal scorecard that people could carry in their shirt pockets or wallets. The scorecard contains three levels of information. The first describes corporate objectives, measures, and targets. The second leaves room for translating corporate targets into targets for each business unit. For the third level, the company asks both individuals and teams to articulate which of their own objectives would be consistent with the business unit and corporate objectives, as well as what initiatives they would take to achieve their objectives. It also asks them to define up to five performance measures for their objectives and to set targets for each measure. The personal scorecard helps to communicate corporate and business unit objectives to the people and teams performing the work, enabling them to translate the objectives into meaningful tasks and targets for themselves. It also lets them keep that information close at hand—in their pockets.

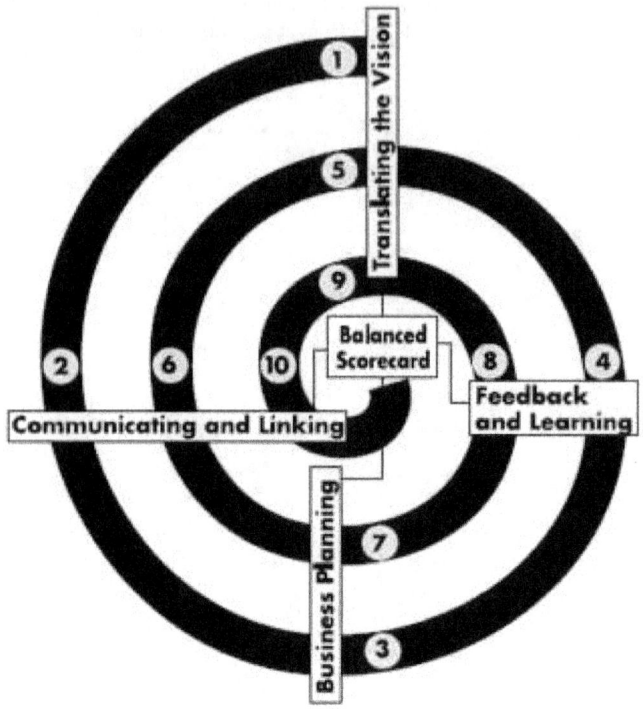

Linking rewards to performance measures. Should compensation systems be linked to balanced scorecard measures? Some companies, believing that tying financial compensation to performance is a powerful lever, have moved quickly to establish such a linkage. For example, an oil company that we'll call Pioneer Petroleum uses its scorecard as the sole basis for computing incentive compensation. The company ties 60% of its executives' bonuses to their achievement of ambitious targets for a weighted average of four financial indicators: return on capital, profitability, cash flow, and operating cost. It bases the remaining 40% on indicators of customer satisfaction, dealer satisfaction, employee satisfaction, and environmental responsibility (such as a percentage change in the level of emissions to water and air). Pioneer's CEO says that linking compensation to the scorecard has helped to align the company with its strategy. "I know of no competitor," he says, "who has this degree of alignment. It is producing results for us."

As attractive and as powerful as such linkage is, it nonetheless carries risks. For instance, does the company have the right measures on the scorecard? Does it have valid and reliable data for the selected measures? Could unintended or unexpected consequences arise from the way the targets for the measures are achieved? Those are questions that companies should ask. Furthermore, companies traditionally handle multiple objectives in a compensation formula by assigning weights to each objective and calculating incentive compensation by the extent to which each weighted objective was achieved. This practice permits substantial incentive compensation to be paid if the business unit overachieves on a few objectives even if it falls far short on others. A better approach would be to establish minimum threshold levels for a critical subset of the strategic measures. Individuals would earn no incentive compensation if performance in a given period fell short of any threshold. This requirement should motivate people to achieve a more balanced performance across short- and long-term objectives.

Some organizations, however, have reduced their emphasis on short-term, formula-based incentive systems as a result of introducing the balanced scorecard. They have discovered that dialogue among executives and managers about the scorecard—both the formulation of the measures and objectives and the explanation of actual versus targeted results—provides a better opportunity to observe managers' performance and abilities. Increased knowledge of their managers' abilities makes it easier for executives to set incentive rewards subjectively and to defend those subjective evaluations—a process that is less susceptible to the game playing and distortions associated with explicit, formula-based rules.

One company we have studied takes an intermediate position. It bases bonuses for business unit managers on two equally weighted criteria: their achievement of a financial objective—economic value added— over a three-year period and a subjective assessment of their performance on measures drawn from the customer, internal-businessprocess, and learning-and-growth perspectives of the balanced scorecard.

That the balanced scorecard has a role to play in the determination of incentive compensation is not in doubt. Precisely what that role should be will become clearer as more companies experiment with linking rewards to scorecard measures.

The Personal Scorecard

Business Planning. "Where the rubber meets the sky": That's how one senior executive describes his company's long-range-planning process. He might have said the same of many other companies because their financially based management systems fail to link change programs and resource allocation to long-term strategic priorities.

The problem is that most organizations have separate procedures and organizational units for strategic planning and for resource allocation and budgeting. To formulate their strategic plans, senior executives go off-site annually and engage for several days in active discussions facilitated by senior planning and development managers or external consultants. The outcome of this exercise is a strategic plan articulating where the company expects (or hopes or prays) to be in three, five, and ten years. Typically, such plans then sit on executives' bookshelves for the next 12 months.

Meanwhile, a separate resource-allocation and budgeting process run by the finance staff sets financial targets for revenues, expenses, profits, and investments for the next fiscal year. The budget it produces consists almost entirely of financial numbers that generally bear little relation to the targets in the strategic plan.

Which document do corporate managers discuss in their monthly and quarterly meetings during the following year? Usually only the budget, because the periodic reviews focus on a comparison of actual and budgeted results for every line item. When is the strategic plan next discussed? Probably during the next annual off-site meeting, when the senior managers draw up a new set of three-, five-, and ten-year plans.

The very exercise of creating a balanced scorecard forces companies to integrate their strategic planning and budgeting processes and therefore helps to ensure that their budgets support their strategies. Scorecard users select measures of progress from all four scorecard perspectives and set targets for each of them. Then they determine which actions will drive them toward their targets, identify the measures they will apply to those drivers from the four perspectives, and establish the short-term milestones that will mark their progress along the strategic paths they have selected. Building a scorecard thus enables a company to link its financial budgets with ist strategic goals.

For example, one division of the Style Company (not its real name) committed to achieving a seemingly impossible goal articulated by the CEO: to double revenues in five years. The forecasts built into the organization's existing strategic plan fell $1 billion short of this objective. The division's managers, after considering various scenarios, agreed to specific increases in five different performance drivers: the number of new stores opened, the number of new customers attracted into new and existing stores, the percentage of shoppers in each store converted into actual purchasers, the portion of existing customers retained, and average sales per customer.

Corporate Objectives
- Double our corporate value in seven years.
- Increase our earnings by an average of 20% per year.
- Achieve an internal rate of return 2% above the cost of capital.
- Increase both production and reserves by 20% in the next decade.

Corporate Targets	Scorecard Measures	Business Unit Targets	Team/Individual Objectives and Initiatives
1995 1996 1997 1998 1999		1995 1996 1997 1998 1999	1
	Financial		
100 120 160 180 250	Earnings [in $ millions]		
100 450 200 210 225	Net cash flow		
100 85 80 75 70	Overhead and operating expenses		2
	Operating		
100 75 73 70 64	Production costs per barrel		
100 97 93 90 82	Development costs per barrel		
100 105 108 108 110	Total annual production		3
Team/Individual Measures		**Targets**	
1			
2			
3			4
4			
5			
Name			
Location			5

By helping to define the key drivers of revenue growth and by committing to targets for each of them, the division's managers eventually grew comfortable with the CEO's ambitious goal.

The process of building a balanced scorecard—clarifying the strategic objectives and then identifying the few critical drivers—also creates a framework for managing an organization's various change programs. These initiatives—reengineering, employee empowerment, time-based management, and total quality management, among others—promise to deliver results but also compete with one another for scarce resources, including the scarcest resource of all: senior managers' time and attention. Shortly after the merger that created it, Metro Bank, for example, launched more than 70 different initiatives. The initiatives were intended to produce a more competitive and successful institution, but they were inadequately integrated into the overall strategy. After building their balanced scorecard, Metro Bank's managers dropped many of those programs—such as a marketing effort directed at individuals with very high net worth—and consolidated others into initiatives that were better aligned with the company's strategic objectives. For example, the managers replaced a program aimed at enhancing existing low-level selling skills with a major initiative aimed at retraining salespersons to become trusted financial advisers, capable of selling a broad range of newly introduced products to the three selected customer segments. The bank made both changes because the scorecard enabled it to gain a better understanding of the programs required to achieve its strategic objectives.

Once the strategy is defined and the drivers are identified, the scorecard influences managers to concentrate on improving or reengineering those processes most critical to the organization's strategic success. That is how the scorecard most clearly links and aligns action with strategy.

The final step in linking strategy to actions is to establish specific short-term targets, or milestones, for the balanced scorecard measures. Milestones are tangible expressions of managers' beliefs about when and to what degree their current programs will affect those measures.

In establishing milestones, managers are expanding the traditional budgeting process to incorporate strategic as well as financial goals. Detailed financial planning remains important, but financial goals taken by themselves ignore the three other balanced scorecard perspectives. In an integrated planning and budgeting process, executives continue to budget for short-term financial performance, but they also introduce shortterm targets for measures in the customer, internal-business-process, and learning-andgrowth perspectives. With those milestones established, managers can continually test both the theory underlying the strategy and the strategy's implementation.

At the end of the business-planning process, managers should have set targets for the long-term objectives they would like to achieve in all four scorecard perspectives; they should have identified the strategic initiatives required and allocated the necessary resources to those initiatives; and they should have established milestones for the measures that mark progress toward achieving their strategic goals.

Feedback and Learning. "With the balanced scorecard," a CEO of an engineering company told us, "I can continually test my strategy. It's like performing real-time research." That is exactly the capability that the scorecard should give senior managers: the ability to know at any point in its implementation whether the strategy they have formulated is, in fact, working, and if not, why.

The first three management processes—translating the vision, communicating and linking, and business planning—are vital for implementing strategy, but they are not sufficient in an unpredictable world. Together they form an important single-loop-learning process—single-loop in the sense that the objective remains constant, and any departure from the planned trajectory is seen as a defect to be remedied. This single-loop process does not require or even facilitate reexamination of either the strategy or the techniques used to implement it in light of current conditions.

Most companies today operate in a turbulent environment with complex strategies that, though valid when they were launched, may lose their validity as business conditions change. In this kind of environment, where new threats and opportunities arise constantly, companies must become capable of what Chris Argyris calls double-loop learning—learning that produces a change in people's assumptions and theories about cause-and-effect relationships.

Budget reviews and other financially based management tools cannot engage senior executives in double-loop learning—first, because these tools address performance from only one perspective, and second, because they don't involve strategic learning. Strategic learning consists of gathering feedback, testing the hypotheses on which strategy was based, and making the necessary adjustments.

The balanced scorecard supplies three elements that are essential to strategic learning. First, it articulates the company's shared vision, defining in clear and operational terms the results that the company, as a team, is trying to achieve. The scorecard communicates a holistic model that links individual efforts and accomplishments to business unit objectives.

Second, the scorecard supplies the essential strategic feedback system. A business strategy can be viewed as a set of hypotheses about cause-and-effect relationships. A strategic feedback system should be able to test, validate, and modify the hypotheses embedded in a business unit's strategy. By establishing short-term goals, or milestones, within the business-planning process, executives are forecasting the relationship between changes in performance drivers and the associated changes in one or more specified goals. For example, executives at Metro Bank estimated the amount of time it would take for improvements in training and in the availability of information systems before employees could sell multiple financial products effectively to existing and new customers. They also estimated how great the effect of that selling capability would be.

Another organization attempted to validate its hypothesized cause-and-effect relationships in the balanced scorecard by measuring the strength of the linkages among measures in the different perspectives. The company found significant correlations between employees' morale, a measure in the learning-and-growth perspective, and customer satisfaction, an important customer perspective measure. Customer satisfaction, in turn, was correlated with faster payment of invoices—a relationship that led to a substantial reduction in accounts receivable and hence a higher return on capital employed. The company also found correlations between employees' morale and the number of suggestions made by employees (two learning-and-growth measures) as well as between an increased number of suggestions and lower rework (an internalbusiness-process measure). Evidence of such strong correlations help to confirm the organization's business strategy. If, however, the expected correlations are not found over time, it should be an indication to executives that the theory underlying the unit's strategy may not be working as they had anticipated.

Especially in large organizations, accumulating sufficient data to document significant correlations and causation among balanced scorecard measures can take a long time—months or years. Over the short term, managers' assessment of strategic impact may have to rest on subjective and qualitative judgments. Eventually, however, as more evidence accumulates, organizations may be able to provide more objectively grounded estimates of cause-and-effect relationships. But just getting managers to think systematically about the assumptions underlying their strategy is an improvement over the current practice of making decisions based on short-term operational results.

Third, the scorecard facilitates the strategy review that is essential to strategic learning. Traditionally, companies use the monthly or quarterly meetings between corporate and division executives to analyze the most recent period's financial results. Discussions focus on past performance and on explanations of why financial objectives were not achieved. The balanced scorecard, with its specification of the causal relationships between performance drivers and objectives, allows corporate and business unit executives to use their periodic review sessions to evaluate the validity of the unit's strategy and the quality of its execution. If the unit's employees and managers have delivered on the performance drivers (retraining of employees, availability of information systems, and new financial products and services, for instance), then their failure to achieve the expected outcomes (higher sales to targeted customers, for example) signals that the theory underlying the strategy may not be valid. The disappointing sales figures are an early warning.

Managers should take such disconfirming evidence seriously and reconsider their shared conclusions about market conditions, customer value propositions, competitors' behavior, and internal capabilities. The result of such a review may be a decision to reaffirm their belief in the current strategy but to adjust the quantitative relationship among the strategic measures on the balanced scorecard. But they also might conclude that the unit needs a different strategy (an example of double-loop learning) in light of new knowledge about market conditions and internal capabilities. In any case, the scorecard will have stimulated key executives to learn about the viability of their strategy. This capacity for enabling organizational learning at the executive level—strategic learning—is what distinguishes the balanced scorecard, making it invaluable for those who wish to create a strategic management system.

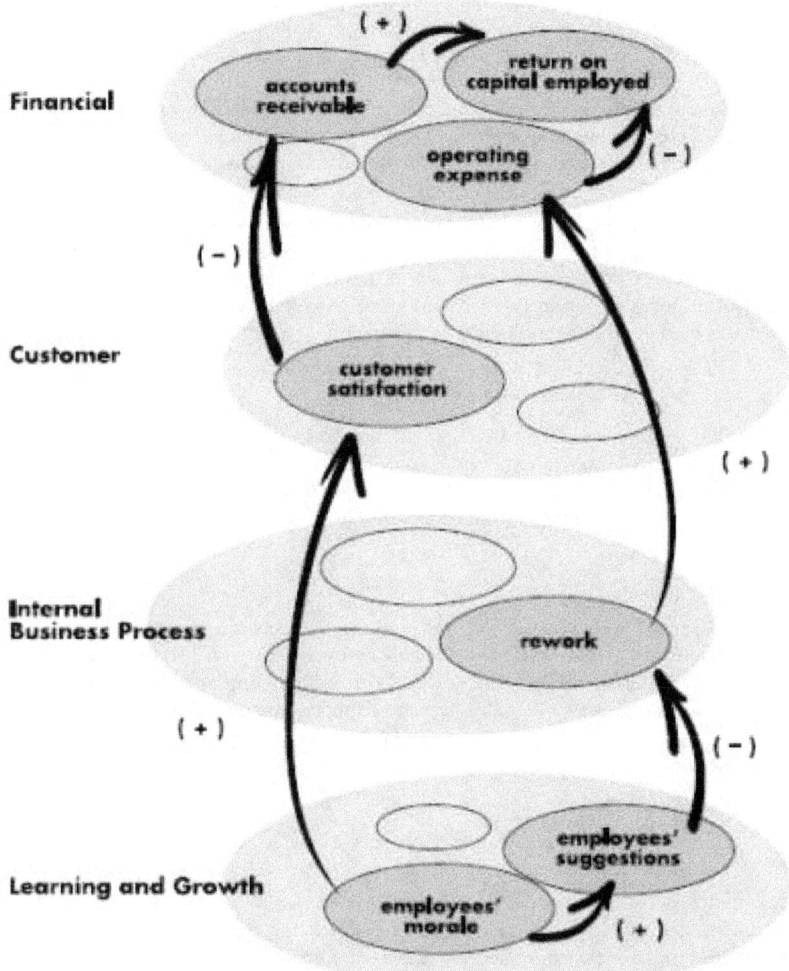

How One Company Linked Measures from the Four Perspectives Toward a New Strategic Management System. Many companies adopted early balanced scorecard concepts to improve their performance measurement systems. They achieved tangible but narrow results. Adopting those concepts provided clarification, consensus, and focus on the desired improvements in performance. More recently, we have seen companies expand their use of the balanced scorecard, employing it as the foundation of an integrated and iterative strategic management system. Companies are using the scorecard to

- clarify and update strategy;
- communicate strategy throughout the company;
- align unit and individual goals with the strategy;
- link strategic objectives to long-term targets and annual budgets;
- identify and align strategic initiatives; and
- conduct periodic performance reviews to learn about and improve strategy.

The balanced scorecard enables a company to align its management processes and focuses the entire organization on implementing long-term strategy. At National Insurance, the scorecard provided the CEO and his managers with a central framework around which they could redesign each piece of the company's management system. And because of the cause-and-effect linkages inherent in the scorecard framework, changes in one component of the system reinforced earlier changes made elsewhere. Therefore, every change made over the 30-month period added to the momentum that kept the organization moving forward in the agreedupon direction.

Without a balanced scorecard, most organizations are unable to achieve a similar consistency of vision and action as they attempt to change direction and introduce new strategies and processes. The balanced scorecard provides a framework for managing the implementation of strategy while also allowing the strategy itself to evolve in response to changes in the company's competitive, market, and technological environments.

The Idea in Brief

Why do budgets often bear little direct relation to a company's long-term strategic objectives? Because they don't take enough into consideration. A balanced scorecard augments traditional financial measures with benchmarks for performance in three key nonfinancial areas: a company's relationship with ist customers

- its key internal processes
- its learning and growth.

When performance measures for these areas are added to the financial metrics, the result is not only a broader perspective on the company's health and activities, it's also a powerful organizing framework. A sophisticated instrument panel for coordinating and fine-tuning a company's operations and businesses so that all activities are aligned with its strategy.

The balanced scorecard relies on four processes to bind short-term activities to long-term objectives:

TRANSLATING THE VISION.

By relying on measurement, the scorecard forces managers to come to agreement on the metrics they will use to operationalize their lofty visions.

Example: A bank had articulated its strategy as providing "superior service to targeted customers." But the process of choosing operational measures for the four areas of the scorecard made executives realize that they first needed to reconcile divergent views of who the targeted customers were and what constituted superior service.

COMMUNICATING AND LINKING.

When a scorecard is disseminated up and down the organizational chart, strategy becomes a tool available to everyone. As the high-level scorecard cascades down to individual business units, overarching strategic objectives and measures are translated into objectives and measures appropriate to each particular group. Tying these targets to individual performance and compensation systems yields "personal scorecards." Thus, individual employees understand how their own productivity supports the overall strategy.

BUSINESS PLANNING.

Most companies have separate procedures (and sometimes units) for strategic planning and budgeting. Little wonder, then, that typical long-term planning is, in the words of one executive, where "the rubber meets the sky." The discipline of creating a balanced scorecard forces companies to integrate the two functions, thereby ensuring that financial budgets do indeed support strategic goals. After agreeing on performance measures for the four scorecard perspectives, companies identify the most influential "drivers" of the desired outcomes and then set milestones for gauging the progress they make with these drivers.

FEEDBACK AND LEARNING.

By supplying a mechanism for strategic feedback and review, the balanced scorecard helps an organization foster a kind of learning often missing in companies: the ability to reflect on inferences and adjust theories about cause-and-effect relationships.

Feedback about products and services. New learning about key internal processes. Technological discoveries. All this information can be fed into the scorecard, enabling strategic refinements to be made continually. Thus, at any point in the implementation, managers can know whether the strategy is working—and if not, why.

CHAPTER 8

What's Wrong with Strategy?

Over the past two decades, the strategic plan has become almost as common a management tool as the budget. But few executives are satisfied with it. Many planning sessions result in no new actions, and the plans themselves often end up buried in bottom drawers. Most planning processes are met with groans rather than cheers.

The popular management author Tom Peters is famous for having offered $100 to the first manager who could demonstrate that a successful strategy had resulted from a planning process. He has never paid out. So what is wrong with strategy or the way we develop strategy?

First, we misuse objectives. We fail to distinguish between *purpose* (what an organization exists to do) and *constraints* (what an organization must do in order to survive). That confusion results in directionless strategies.

Second, we are confounded by process. Objectives are intertwined with strategy and with implementation in a way that makes it difficult for an organization to decide where to start. Should managers set objectives and develop strategies to achieve them? Or should they look for a winning strategy and then carve objectives out of their understanding of what is achievable? Such confusion about where to begin causes planning paralysis. Third, we expect that planning processes will lead to new and improvedstrategies. But the basic ingredient of a good strategy – insight into how to create value – rarely emerges from planning meetings. Instead, it originates in many varied and hard-to-control ways, some of which are more about implementation than about strategy development. Thus managers who focus on planning processes often create flatfooted plans.

The answer to developing a good strategy is not new planning processes or better-designed plans. The answer lies in managers' understanding two fundamental points: the benefit of having a well-articulated, stable purpose, and the importance of discovering, understanding, documenting, and exploiting insights about how to create more value than other companies do.

Objectives: Purpose or Constraint? It is much easier for a company to develop a plan if it knows what it's trying to achieve. Clear objectives are a necessary part of good plan ning. But what objectives should a company have? The advice to managers on this topic is often confusing. They are encouraged to come up with vision statements, mission statements, strategic intent, shareholder- value objectives, and customer focus.

Managers at the business-unit level frequently complain that the company's objectives are not clear. A common refrain is, "Why doesn't corporate tell us what it wants us to do? Then we can devote our energies to figuring out how to do it." The tension is often between financial goals, such as cash flow and profit, and strategic goals, such as market position and growth.

At the corporate level, the problem of having unclear objectives is usually addressed with the mantra of shareholder value. "Our objective is to provide a superior return to our shareholders," proclaim many annual reports. Some companies have a clear profit or size target for the year 2000 or 2005. Others have a stakeholder statement explaining that the company will provide superior returns to shareholders, better value to customers, and above-market salaries and career opportunities to employees.

Why are those stakeholder objectives unsatisfactory? Why don't they make strategy development easier? The answer is that such objectives do little more than restate the rules of the economic game that companies play. They provide no help to the strategist in any given company because they are just a different way of defining the universal objective of all companies: to develop and sustain competitive advantage.

The stakeholder model is helpful in explaining the rules of the economic game and the link between stakeholder value and competitive advantage. (See the chart "The Role of Stakeholders in Strategy.") Companies must win and retain some loyalty from each of their active stakeholders: shareholders, customers, employees, and suppliers. Without support from all four groups, companies cannot function– they cannot finance themselves, sell their products, recruit suitable employees, or purchase the supplies they need. These stakeholders are active not just because they have a commercial relationship with the company but also because they are infinitely greedy: they want to get as much as possible out of the relationship. Their greed is fueled by the existence of competitors.

Even suppliers – normally considered the most passive of the stakeholders – are comparing the benefits of dealing with company A with those of dealing with company B. If a supplier views its relationship with company B as being more valuable than its relationship with company A, it will provide company B with more attention, better deliveries, higher-quality components, and faster responses on rush orders. Employees also make such comparisons, weighing the advantages of their current jobs with the benefits of other possibilities for employment. And customers – often viewed as the most active stakeholders –regularly compare a company with its competitors and often buy from them just to see what their products and services are like. Finally, shareholders compare the results of their investments in a company with opportunities in similar sectors that have similar risk profiles.

In other words, stakeholders in our economic system are being actively wooed all the time by competitors. A company must give a stream of value to each stakeholder that the stakeholder views as being at least as good as the stream of value offered by competitors, taking into account switching costs. If stakeholders do not perceive such value, they will redirect their loyalty, either gradually or precipitously. Seen in this light, creating stakeholder value is not so much an *objective* as it is an *economic constraint* on a company's actions. If, for example, a company takes actions that fail to deliver sufficient shareholder value, it will lose the loyalty of its shareholders and as a result go out of business. The same is true of its relationships with the other active stakeholders.

There are other, less active stakeholders, such as governments, communities, and special interest groups. These other stakeholders are distinguished from the active stakeholders because they are not infinitely greedy. They have specific requirements – constraints that are often fairly easy for companies to live with. In addition, their requirements are demanding but achievable. Consequently, it is not customary for companies to include actions such as paying taxes or obeying the law as part of their objectives.

In contrast, managers often state company objectives in shareholder or customer terms because it can be very difficult to provide these stakeholders with sufficient value – which is always defined in relative terms. If one competitor increases the value it delivers, it raises the hurdle for all other competitors. A company can only afford to deliver sufficient value to all its stakeholders if it has competitive advantage. As a result, our economic system demands that companies have as one of their driving objectives, or constraints, the search for and creation of competitive advantage. That one objective is the link between the stakeholder model and the traditional strategist model. When strategists talk about competitive advantage, they are saying no more than "superior delivery to stakeholders." To describe competitive advantage or stakeholder value as an objective that drives thinking about strategy is to misunderstand these universal constraints. Competitive advantage is a requirement for retaining stakeholders' support over the long term. But recognizing this requirement does not in itself give the strategist any guidance on how to achieve it.

If competitive advantage is a constraint rather than a purpose, what sorts of objectives should companies define as their starting points for strategy? The answer is objectives that describe the essence of why the organization exists. If the organiza tion exists solely to make money for shareholders, then that is its purpose. But such a purpose offers very little guidance about what sort of strategy to follow. If, on the other hand, the organization exists to "make cosmetics that don't hurt animals" (one of the purposes of the Body Shop, for example), then a statement about this objective provides some guidance to strategists. The purpose limits the range of strategic choices that need evaluating and therefore helps to simplify strategy development.

The Role of Stakeholders in Strategy

Many executives mistakenly believe that satisfying stakeholders is an objective that drives thinking about strategy. In fact, it's a constraint, not an objective. Companies that don't win the loyalty of stakeholders will go out of business.

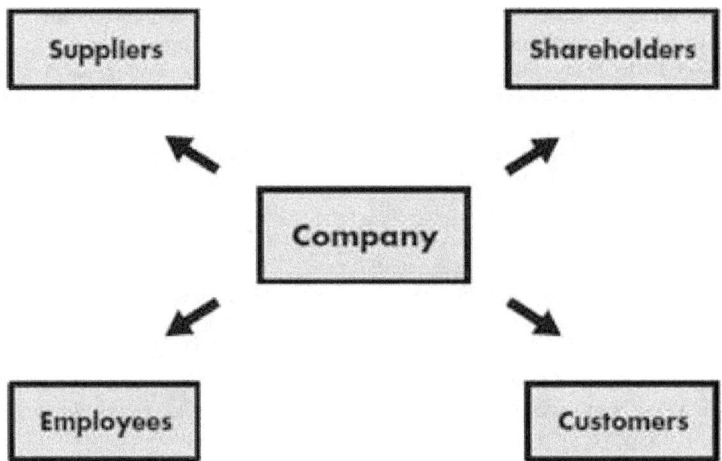

The more focused and detailed a purpose is, the more likely it is that a company will be able to develop a winning strategy. One of the frustrations organizations have with strategic planning stems from the lack of attention given to defining purpose. Paradoxically, allowing too many options for defining purpose makes strategy development more difficult rather than less so.

From Purpose to Strategy. MOST (mission, objectives, strategy, tactics) is an acronym used in many strategy courses. It suggests that there is a structure and order to strategy development that managers should follow. First, strategists should choose a mission – a longterm purpose for the organization. Then they should define short-term and mid-term objectives that will move the organization on a path toward the mission. A strategy can now be developed to achieve the objectives using short-term operating decisions, or tactics, to implement the strategy.

But the process of developing a winning strategy is much more messy, experimental, and iterative; and it is driven from the bottom up. Take, for example, a typical management-team meeting to launch a strategy development process. Let us assume that the managers have defined their mission (or purpose) as follows: "to be a global computer company known for its innovative products and environmental positioning." They are now looking to develop some objectives. One manager suggests an objective of achieving equal sales in Asia, Europe, and the Americas. Another suggests a 50% reduction in the use of chlorine-based plastics, such as polyvinyl chloride. A third argues for a 20% market-share target, which would make the company number two in its market.

Immediately, realism enters into the discussion. Which of these objectives is achievable in a competitive world? Achievability depends on whether the management team can generate a strategy for reaching the objective, taking into account the stakeholder constraints. If the group cannot think of a strategy, it is likely to reject the objective as unrealistic. Which, then, comes first: objectives or strategy? The two are, in fact, intertwined until the moment when a combination of objectives and strategy is chosen.

After a lengthy debate, the management team agrees to make its driving objective a 20% market share and to implement a strategy based on developing new products faster and more effectively than the company's competitors. At that point, market share becomes an objective of the team's strategy, and a target of three new products in the next year becomes an objective for aiding the implementation of the strategy.

Tactics and strategy have the same sequencing problem. The strategy to develop new products faster and more effectively than competitors is viable only if the managers can envision the tactics for its implementation. If the managers know where to recruit additional research staff, see parts of the product development process that can be streamlined, and have ideas about how to involve customers and suppliers more fully in product development, then the strategy is viable. If not, the strategy may not be realistic. Tactics need to be worked out before the strategy can be determined, and the strategy needs to be clear in order to define the objectives. The MOST framework therefore collapses from a sequential path into a simultaneous coming together of the elements.

The problem of where to start causes planning paralysis. Without clear objectives, the task of formulating a strategy seems daunting. Without an agreed-upon strategy, a management team often lacks the energy to work out the tactical details. Yet only an understanding of the tactical details provides the insights for a winning strategy and gives leaders the courage to set bold objectives. Managers who start by setting objectives often meet resistance from those developing the strategy because the strategists cannot find a way to achieve the objectives and, at the same time, satisfy all the stakeholders. Managers who, on the other hand, lead with a clear strategy find that other managers drag their feet because they cannot work out the tactics to implement it. The result in both instances is a form of stalemate in which senior managers demand objectives from their bosses and then declare the objectives to be unrealistic, while junior managers ask for strategies from the senior managers and then find them to be impractical. The solution to this impasse is to understand the fundamental building block of good strategy: insight into how to create more value than competitors can.

Insights into Value Creation. Insights into value creation are understandings about the production and delivery process or about the needs of stakeholders that allow one to discover superior ways of creating value. These insights normally focus on practical issues and point to new ways of doing things. They can be about relationships with suppliers, about the details of the recruitment process or the needs of a particular group of employees, about customer segments, or about the value equations used by shareholders. Sometimes the insights are grand ideas to reconfigure the company or the industry completely. More commonly, they are discoveries that some process can be performed by fewer people or that a segment of customers requires a new service. Such insights often come from line or operating managers who may not be fully aware of their significance.

These points about value creation lead to two important conclusions about strategy and tactics. First, separating strategy formulation from implementation generally is not a good idea. Most of the insights important for strategy formulation reside in the heads of the operating managers. And although operating managers often are not the best strategists, excluding them from strategy development means excluding their insights as well.

Second, tactics are not only about implementing today's strategy but also about discovering tomorrow's strategy. Tomorrow's insights arise from today's operating experiences. Unless implementation is also viewed as being part of strategy development, tomorrow's strategy is likely to be short on insights

Managers at Wimpy noticed that McDonald's restaurants were usually cleaner than Wimpy restaurants. Knowing that cleanliness is critical to the success of fast-food operations, they were eager to raise their standards. Yet despite many experiments, they could not find a way to achieve the McDonald's standard of day-to-day cleanliness without spending an excessive amount on cleaning services. They finally determined that the advantage of McDonald's lay in the attitude of ist staff – their willingness to use any downtime to mop, tidy, and polish.

Were the McDonald's operating procedures a strategy or a tactic? Clearly, the company's operations and culture were giving it a strategic advantage. Where should analysts draw the lines between objectives, strategy, and tactics? And which comes first? Did the managers at McDonald's decide on an objective of cleanliness, develop a cleanliness strategy, and then implement some cultural tactics? Or did the long-standing culture of having staff clean up around them result in more employees concerned about cleanliness, thus creating an environment that was cleaner than that of competitors? Either way, the distinction between objectives, strategy, and tactics is not a useful one. What Wimpy (integrated into the Burger King chain in 1989) needed were some new insights that would enable it to offer customers a better value proposition than McDonald's.

Looking for Insights. Many strategic-planning processes confuse strategy with planning. Plans exist to cope with the immediate needs of the organization. They operate under a preset timetable and demand structured documentation. Planning is a valuable activity and is unfairly derided, but it is a different process from forming strategy. Planning processes are not designed to accommodate the messy process of generating insights and molding them into a winning strategy. A well-structured planning process is therefore likely to be ill suited to strategy formulation.

So how should companies set about developing the insights that will give them exciting yet practical strategies? The answer is, we don't know. Rival camps sell different solutions, but none has been able to demonstrate that its solutions are clearly the best. In fact, since strategy is about insights, almost by definition there is no best way.

If one way of developing insights were best, all competitors would immediately start using it, and we would be back to where we started, searching for new ways to gain advantage over competitors. Hence there is likely to be no long-term solution to the problem. There are only temporary solutions – periods in which only a few companies have processes for generating superior insights. But as the processes become more widely used, they lose their advantage. Failing to use them will be a disadvantage for companies, but using them will not solve the fundamental long-term problem.

It is for this reason that management fads are so faddish. Companies scramble to use the processes used by competitors. Whether it is total quality management, benchmarking, process reengineering, strategic planning, empowerment, core competence analysis, or some other concept, managers are right to experiment with each new fad, even if it is worth little more than snake oil. The penalty for not keeping up with new ways of generating insights can be severe.

Strategists fall into three camps when discussing how to develop insights: those who focus on operating issues, those who focus on gazing into the future, and those who focus on behavior and culture. Some strategists are members of more than one camp, although they often exhibit a strong bias toward one of the three approaches.

The operating camp proclaims the value of such processes as reengineering, time-based competition, benchmarking, total quality management, empowerment, and many other tools for evaluating the effectiveness of today's operations and for finding better ways of doing things. Undoubtedly, these tools and processes produce improvements. Although they rarely lead to great strategies, they have been found to lead to solid, workable strategies that come out of insights gained from solving operating problems. Toyota's development of the *kanban* process, for example, came about when it tried to solve a space problem in its warehouses.

Processes endorsed by the futuregazing camp define the factors critical to future success. Those processes involve choosing which critical factors to focus on and then designing an organization with the appropriate capabilities. Competitive strategy analysis in the Michael Porter mold is one way of defining the critical factors for success. Scenario analysis, a tool used by Shell, is another way of getting at the same outcome. More recently, Gary Hamel and C.K. Prahalad have developed a process and way of thinking that involve many managers in many hundreds of hours of analysis and debate in order to help generate foresight about an industry's direction. At a more mundane level, tools such as Richard Foster's technology S-curve and Motorola's technology maps are popular ways of understanding the future. Finally, chaos theorists are beginning to have an influence. Using the discovery that chaotic systems have stable patterns to which they periodically return, chaos theorists argue that companies should define critical success factors in terms of those stable patterns and ignore the truly chaotic periods in between. Such periods defy analysis, they say.

The behavior-and-culture camp comprises two groups of proponents. The first group is the data-free-planning enthusiasts, who believe that a clear vision is the key to successfully discovering insights. Individuals who can convince themselves that they will achieve an objective and who can clearly imagine that achievement engage something called the creative subconscious. It starts to work overtime to eliminate cognitive dissonance, a form of mental discomfort created by a present situation that is different from the vision. The result is that the individual makes things happen in such a way that the vision becomes a reality and the dissonance is eliminated. Ideas such as Hamel and Prahalad's strategic intent fall into this category, as do the theories of many purveyors of mission and vision thinking. Data-free-planning enthusiasts are trying to operate at the level of the organization as a whole and are attempting to create a cognitive dissonance that harnesses the organization's creative juices.

The second group in the behavior-and-culture camp focuses on organizational learning. Chris Argyris is famous for his double-loop-learning principles and his exposure of defensive routines that prevent learning. He argues that by eliminating those defensive routines, we can open ourselves up to learning and, as a result, become more receptive to new insights. Many others are also working on the idea of a learning organization – a culture in which the development of insights is more likely. Peter Senge, for example, argues that systems thinking is one of the most effective ways to increase learning and develop more insights.

In view of the radically different ideas about how to develop insights, and the requirement of a simultaneous rather than a sequential alignment of objectives, strategy, and tactics, it is not surprising that managers become confused and disheartened. No one can blame them for seizing on the planning process as an alternative to strategy development. It appears to be a manageable path through the turbid swamp of strategy making. But it is a slippery path and offers no ultimate way forward by itself. Progressing through the swamp is not easy, but there are two pieces of firm ground that managers must cling to. If they lose their grip on these two, they will be sucked down rapidly.

Purpose and Insights. Purpose is one of those pieces of firm ground. Strategists need to devote more attention to the issue of purpose and be ready to revisit it whenever they are caught up in circular thinking. Purpose can be highly detailed and thus provide clear direction. It can define the product or technology, the market to be targeted, the type of positioning to be achieved, and the values that must guide behavior. The more detailed the purpose, the more the strategist can focus; at the same time, the more danger there is that the purpose is unrealistic or will quickly change. Purpose may evolve as one moves through the swamp, but if changes to it are frequent or unclear, the firm ground may slip away.

For example, the original purpose of Marks and Spencer, one of the most successful U.K. retailers, was to provide affordable everyday clothing of unrivaled quality to working people. That purpose provided a clear market and product focus and defined the challenge for the company's strategy. For several decades, Marks and Spencer's purpose has extended its product range to food, houseplants, and personal financial services and has shifted the target market toward the upscale. But the theme of being a retailer that sets new standards of quality for massmarket products has provided a consistent, if gradually evolving, focus for Marks and Spencer's strategic development.

Similarly, when Volkswagen was established in 1920, its purpose, as its name – "people's car" – implies, was to create a robust German automobile for the average family. That purpose set a clear challenge for strategy development, which by 1972 had made the Beetle the most popular automobile in the world.

The Body Shop, with its purposes of producing and selling cosmetics that avoid harming animals or the environment, promoting Third World trade, and encouraging responsible entrepreneurship, illustrates the role of values within purpose. Values provide extra focus beyond product-market definition and suggest fruitful avenues for strategy development. Furthermore, strategies that conflict with a company's values should not be entertained by the company.

Purpose becomes more difficult to articulate as a company becomes broader in its scope. When Canon was originally established as the Precision Optical Research Laboratory in 1933, its purpose was to create a Japanese camera that rivaled the Leica. Having achieved that purpose beyond all expectations and moved into new areas such as pocket calculators, Canon was in danger of losing its way. In 1976, Ryuzaburo Kaku (who later became chairman) pulled the company out of the swamp. He was the driving force behind the company's thorough articulation of purpose in the "Premier Company" plan, which started to communicate much broader and more enduring values. This exercise was repeated in 1982, 1988, and subsequently, providing a critical reassertion of what the company was all about. Although Canon's purpose can no longer be as clear-cut as it was in 1933, the effort devoted to clarifying and articulating a purpose has helped the company produce a series of winning strategies.

The best purposes give long-term, directional stability without pushing the organization into an unrealistic box. But strategists should not insist on a purpose if one does not exist. For many large diversified companies, there is no purpose beyond creating shareholder value (that is, playing by the rules). In such circumstances, all possible strategies, including liquidating the business, need to be evaluated – however difficult that may be for strategists.

Insights represent the second piece of firm ground. Strategists need to build their thinking around insights and how to discover them. Insights give meaning to tactics, which in turn make strategies doable and allow objectives to be set with the knowledge that they can, with a fair wind, be achieved.

In strategy formulation, we counsel managers to focus less on the action plan – or even on the articulation of the strategy itself – and more on the insights. We suggest that planning processes are not strategic (and may not even be worth engaging in) unless they focus initially on defining the insights from which the strategy will be developed. The insights about value creation at Marks and Spencer are primarily about the way suppliers are selected and managed and the way employees are treated. This has enabled the company to maintain unusually high control over quality without incurring high costs. The insights at Canon are about how technologies can be combined in more innovative ways. This has led to a string of new products that continue to expand the company's technology base in a virtuous circle. The insights at the Body Shop are about the value that employees and customers attach to natural and environmental products and to morally ambitious organizations. Reduced waste and creative sourcing have led to an advantaged cost structure, to highly motivated staff and franchisees.

It is unlikely that any of those insights emerged from a strategy development exercise any more than Honda's 50cc minibike and famous insights about penetrating the U.S motorcycle market resulted from such exercises. Honda's original strategy, which focused on large, traditional bikes, was not based on any insights and did not work. But having stumbled across the insight that there was latent demand for a new kind of motorbike in the United States, Honda soon found a viable strategy for exploiting that demand.

If a company can come up with true insights, then developing a strategy to exploit them is a viable task. Developing a strategy without insights is dangerous because it leads to unrealistic plans. The best approach is to move through the swamp in search of firm ground. But in this search process, it is tempting to confuse struggling forward in some arbitrary direction with having a strategy. That confusion hampers the search and reduces the organization's chances of recognizing firm ground when it encounters it.

Defining purpose, discovering insights, and combining the two into a strategy is not easy. All three steps are hard, which is why the strategy development puzzle frequently doesn't get solved. But the puzzle is made more difficult if we fail to distinguish between purpose and constraint, if we doggedly put objectives before strategy and strategy before tactics, and if we design structured planning processes with timetables that do not allow for the discovery of new insights. By defining purpose and insight as the two islands of substance in the strategy swamp, managers have a better chance of progressing toward the winning strategy they are all striving for.

CHAPTER 9

Why Good Projects Fail Anyway

When a promising project doesn't deliver, chances are the problem wasn't the idea but how it was carried out. Here's a way to design projects that guards against unnecessary failure. By Nadim F. Matta and Ronald N. Ashkenas

Big projects fail at an astonishing rate. Whether major technology installations, postmerger integrations, or new growth strategies, these efforts consume tremendous resources over months or even years. Yet as study after study has shown, they frequently deliver disappointing returns by some estimates, in fact, well over half the time. And the toll they take is not just financial. These failures demoralize employees who have labored diligently to complete their share of the work. One middle manager at a top pharmaceutical company told us, "I've been on dozens of task teams in my career, and I've never actually seen one that produced a result."

The problem is, the traditional approach to project management shifts the project teams' focus away from the end result toward developing recommendations, new technologies, and partial solutions. The intent, of course, is to piece these together into a blueprint that will achieve the ultimate goal, but when a project involves many people working over an extended period of time, it's very hard for managers planning it to predict all the activities and work streams that will be needed. Unless the end product is very well understood, as it is in highly technical engineering projects such as building an airplane, it's almost inevitable that some things will be left off the plan. And even if all the right activities have been anticipated, they may turn out to be difficult, or even impossible, to knit together once they're completed.

Managers use project plans, timelines, and budgets to reduce what we call "execution risk"— the risk that designated activities won't be carried out properly—but they inevitably neglect these two other critical risks—the "white space risk" that some required activities won't be identified in advance, leaving gaps in the project plan, and the "integration risk" that the disparate activities won't come together at the end. So project teams can execute their tasks flawlessly, on time and under budget, and yet the overall project may still fail to deliver the intended results.

We've worked with hundreds of teams over the past 20 years, and we've found that by designing complex projects differently, managers can reduce the likelihood that critical activities will be left off the plan and increase the odds that all the pieces can be properly integrated at the end. The key is to inject into the overall plan a series of miniprojects—what we call *rapid-results initiatives* —each staffed with a team responsible for a version of the hoped-for overall result in miniature and each designed to deliver its result quickly.

Let's see what difference that would make. Say, for example, your goal is to double sales revenue over two years by implementing a customer relationship management (CRM) system for your sales force. Using a traditional project management approach, you might have one team research and install software packages, another analyze the different ways that the company interacts with customers (e-mail, telephone, and in person, for example), another develop training programs, and so forth. Many months later, however, when you start to roll out the program, you might discover that the salespeople aren't sold on the benefits. So even though they may know how to enter the requisite data into the system, they refuse. This very problem has, in fact, derailed many CRM programs at major organizations.

But consider the way the process might unfold if the project included some rapid-results initiatives. A single team might take responsibility for helping a small number of users—say, one sales group in one region—increase their revenues by 25% within four months. Team members would probably draw on all the activities described above, but to succeed at their goal, the microcosm of the overall goal, they would be forced to find out what, if anything, is missing from their plans as they go forward. Along the way, they would, for example, discover the salespeople's resistance, and they would be compelled to educate the sales staff about the system's benefits. The team may also discover that it needs to tackle other issues, such as how to divvy up commissions on sales resulting from cross-selling or joint-selling efforts.

When they've ironed out all the kinks on a small scale, their work would then become a model for the next teams, which would either engage in further rapid-results initiatives or roll the system out to the whole organization but now with a higher level of confidence that the project will have the intended impact on sales revenue. The company would see an early payback on its investment and gain new insights from the team's work, and the team would have the satisfaction of delivering real value.

In the pages that follow, we'll take a close look at rapid-results initiatives, using case studies to show how these projects are selected and designed and how they are managed in conjunction with more traditional project activities.

How Rapid-Results Teams Work. Let's look at an extremely complex project, a World Bank initiative begun in June 2000 that aims to improve the productivity of 120,000 small-scale farmers in Nicaragua by 30% in 16 years. A project of this magnitude entails many teams working over a long period of time, and it crosses functional and organizational boundaries.

They started as they had always done: A team of World Bank experts and their clients in the country (in this case, Ministry of Agriculture officials) spent many months in preparation—conducting surveys, analyzing data, talking to people with comparable experiences in other countries, and so on. Based on their findings, these project strategists, designers, and planners made an educated guess about the major streams of work that would be required to reach the goal. These work streams included reorganizing government institutions that give technical advice to farmers, encouraging the creation of a private-sector market in agricultural support services (such as helping farmers adopt new farming technologies and use improved seeds), strengthening the National Institute for Agricultural Technology (INTA), and establishing an information management system that would help agricultural R&D institutions direct their efforts to the most productive areas of research. The result of all this preparation was a multiyear project plan, a document laying out the work streams in detail.

But if the World Bank had kept proceeding in the traditional way on a project of this magnitude, it would have been years before managers found out if something had been left off the plan or if the various work streams could be integrated—and thus if the project would ultimately achieve its goals. By that time, millions of dollars would have been invested and much time potentially wasted. What's more, even if everything worked according to plan, the project's beneficiaries would have been waiting for years before seeing any payoff from the effort. As it happened, the project activities proceeded on schedule, but a new minister of agriculture came on board two years in and argued that he needed to see results sooner than the plan allowed. His complaint resonated with Norman Piccioni, the World Bank team leader, who was also getting impatient with the project's pace. As he said at the time, "Apart from the minister, the farmers, and me, I'm not sure anyone working on this project is losing sleep over whether farmer productivity will be improved or not."

Over the next few months, we worked with Piccioni to help him and his clients add rapidresults initiatives to the implementation process. They launched five teams, which included not only representatives from the existing work streams but also the beneficiaries of the project, the farmers themselves. The teams differed from traditional implementation teams in three fundamental ways. Rather than being partial, horizontal, and long term, they were results oriented, vertical, and fast. A look at each attribute in turn shows why they were more effective.

Results Oriented. As the name suggests, a rapid-results initiative is intentionally commissioned to produce a measurable result, rather than recommendations, analyses, or partial solutions. And even though the goal is on a smaller scale than the overall objective, it is nonetheless challenging. In Nicaragua, one team's goal was to increase Grade A milk production in the Leon municipality from 600 to 1,600 gallons per day in 120 days in 60 small and medium-size producers. Another was to increase pig weight on 30 farms by 30% in 100 days using enhanced corn seed. A third was to secure commitments from private-sector experts to provide technical advice and agricultural support to 150 small-scale farmers in the El Sauce (the dry farming region) within 100 days.

This results orientation is important for three reasons. First, it allows project planners to test whether the activities in the overall plan will add up to the intended result and to alter the plans if need be. Second, it produces real benefits in the short term. Increasing pig weight in 30 farms by 30% in just over three months is useful to those 30 farmers no matter what else happens in the project. And finally, being able to deliver results is more rewarding and energizing for teams than plodding along through partial solutions.

The focus on results also distinguishes rapidresults initiatives from pilot projects, which are used in traditionally managed initiatives only to reduce execution risk. Pilots typically are designed to test a preconceived solution, or means, such as a CRM system, and to work out implementation details before rollout. Rapidresults initiatives, by contrast, are aimed squarely at reducing white space and integration risk.

Vertical. Project plans typically unfold as a series of activities represented on a timeline by horizontal bars. In this context, rapid-results initiatives are vertical. They encompass a slice of several horizontal activities, implemented in tandem in a very short time frame. By using the term "vertical," we also suggest a cross-functional effort, since different horizontal work streams usually include people from different parts of an organization (or even, as in Nicaragua, different organizations), and the vertical slice brings these people together. This vertical orientation is key to reducing white space and integration risks in the overall effort: Only by uncovering and properly integrating any activities falling in the white space between the horizontal project streams will the team be able to deliver its miniresult.

The team working on securing commitments between farmers and technical experts in the dry farming region, for example, had to knit together a broad set of activities. The experts needed to be trained to deliver particular services that the farmers were demanding because they had heard about new ways to increase their productivity through the information management system. That, in turn, was being fed information coming out of INTA's R&D efforts, which were directed toward addressing specific problems the farmers had articulated. So team members had to draw on a number of the broad horizontal activities laid out in the overall project plan and integrate them into their vertical effort. As they did so, they discovered that they had to add activities missing from the original horizontal work streams. Despite the team members' heroic efforts to integrate the ongoing activities, for instance, 80 days into their 100-day initiative, they had secured only half the commitments they were aiming for. Undeterred and spurred on by the desire to accomplish their goal, team members drove through the towns of the region announcing with loudspeakers the availability and benefits of the technical services. Over the following 20 days, the gap to the goal was closed. To close the white space in the project plan, "marketing of technical services" was added as another horizontal stream.

Fast. How fast is fast? Rapid-results projects generally last no longer than 100 days. But they are by no means quick fixes, which imply shoddy or short-term solutions. And while they deliver quick wins, the more important value of these initiatives is that they change the way teams approach their work. The short time frame fosters a sense of personal challenge, ensuring that team members feel a sense of urgency right from the start that leaves no time to squander on big studies or interorganizational bickering. In traditional horizontal work streams, the gap between current status and the goal starts out far wider, and a feeling of urgency does not build up until a short time before the day of reckoning. Yet it is precisely at that point that committed teams kick into a high-creativity mode and begin to experiment with new ideas to get results. That kick comes right away in rapid-results initiatives.

A Shift in Accountability. In most complex projects, the executives shaping and assigning major work streams assume the vast majority of the responsibility for the project's success. They delegate execution risk to project teams, which are responsible for staying on time and on budget, but they inadvertently leave themselves carrying the full burden of white space and integration risk. In World Bank projects, as in most complex and strategically critical efforts, these risks can be huge.

When executives assign a team responsibility for a result, however, the team is free—indeed, compelled—to find out what activities will be needed to produce the result and how those activities will fit together. This approach puts white space and integration risk onto the shoulders of the people doing the work. That's appropriate because, as they work, they can discover on the spot what's working and what's not. And in the end, they are rewarded not for performing a series of tasks but for delivering real value. Their success is correlated with benefits to the organization, which will come not only from implementing known activities but also from identifying and integrating new activities.

The milk productivity team in Nicaragua, for example, found out early on that the quantity of milk production was not the issue. The real problem was quality: Distributors were being forced to dump almost half the milk they had bought due to contamination, spoilage, and other problems. So the challenge was to produce milk acceptable to large distributors and manufacturers that complied with international quality standards. Based on this understanding, the team leader invited a representative of Parmalat, the biggest private company in Nicaragua's dairy sector, to join the team. Collaborating with this customer allowed the team to understand Parmalat's quality standards and thus introduce proper hygiene practices to the milk producers in Leon. The collaboration also identified the need for simple equipment such as a centrifuge that could test the quality of batches quickly.

The quality of milk improved steadily in the initial stage of the effort. But then the team discovered that its goal of tripling sales was in danger due to a logistics problem: There wasn't adequate storage available for the additional Grade A milk now being produced. Rather than invest in refrigeration facilities, the Parmalat team member (now assured of the quality of the milk) suggested that the company conduct collection runs in the area daily rather than twice weekly.

At the end of 120 days, the milk productivity team (renamed the "clean-milking" team) and the other four teams not only achieved their goals but also generated a new appreciation for the discovery process. As team leader Piccioni observed at a follow-up workshop: "I now realize how much of the overall success of the effort depends on people discovering for themselves what goals to set and what to do to achieve them."

What's more, the work is more rewarding for the people involved. It may seem paradoxical, but virtually all the teams we've encountered prefer to work on projects that have results-oriented goals, even though they involve some risk and require some discovery, rather than implement clearly predefined tasks.

The Leadership Balancing Act. Despite the obvious benefits of rapid-results initiatives, few companies should use them to replace the horizontal activities altogether. Because of their economies of scale, horizontal activities are a cost-efficient way to work. And so it is the job of the leadership team to balance rapid-results initiatives with longterm horizontal activities, help spread insights from team to team, and blend everything into an overall implementation strategy.

In Nicaragua, the vertical teams drew members from the horizontal teams, but these people continued to work on the horizontal streams as well, and each team benefited from the work of the others. So, for example, when the milk productivity team discovered the need to educate farmers in clean-milking practices, the horizontal training team knew to adjust the design of its overall training programs accordingly.

The adhesive-material and office-product company Avery Dennison took a similar approach, creating a portfolio of rapid-results initiatives and horizontal work streams as the basis for its overall growth acceleration strategy. Just over a year ago, the company was engaged in various horizontal activities like new technology investments and market studies. The company was growing, but CEO Phil Neal and his leadership team were not satisfied with the pace. Although growth was a major corporate goal, the company had increased its revenues by only 8% in two years.

In August 2002, Neal and president Dean Scarborough tested the vertical approach in three North American divisions, launching 15 rapid-results teams in a matter of weeks. One was charged with securing one new order for an enhanced product, refined in collaboration with one large customer, within 100 days. Another focused on signing up three retail chains so it could use that experience to develop a methodology for moving into new distribution channels. A third aimed to book several hundred thousand dollars in sales in 100 days by providing—through a collaboration with three other suppliers—all the parts needed by a major customer. By December, it had become clear that the vertical growth initiatives were producing results, and the management team decided to extend the process throughout the company, supported by an extensive employee communication campaign. The horizontal activities continued, but at the same time dozens of teams, involving hundreds of people, started working on rapid-results initiatives. By the end of the first quarter of 2003, these teams yielded more than $8 million in new sales, and the company was forecasting that the initiatives would realize approximately $50 million in sales by the end of the year.

The Diversified Products business of Zurich North America, a division of Zurich Financial Services, has taken a similarly strategic approach. CEO Rob Fishman and chief underwriting officer Gary Kaplan commissioned and launched dozens of rapid-results initiatives between April 1999 and December 2002. Their overall long-term objectives were to improve their financial performance and strengthen relationships with core clients. And so they combined vertical teams focused on such goals as increasing payments from a small number of clients for value-added services with horizontal activities targeting staff training, internal processes, and the technology infrastructure. The results were dramatic: In less than four years, loss ratios in the property side of the business dropped by 90%, the expense ratio was cut in half, and fees for value-added services increased tenfold.

Now, when you're managing a portfolio of vertical initiatives and horizontal activities, one of the challenges becomes choosing where to focus the verticals. We generally advise company executives to identify aspects of the effort that they're fairly sure will fail if they are not closely coordinated with one another. We also engage the leadership team in a discussion aimed at identifying other areas of potential uncertainty or risk. Based on those discussions, we ask executives to think of projects that could replicate their longer-term goals on a small scale in a short time and provide the maximum opportunity for learning and discovery.

For instance, at Johnson & Johnson's pharmaceutical R&D group, Thomas Kirsch, the head of global quality assurance, needed to integrate the QA functions for two traditionally autonomous clinical R&D units whose people were located around the world. Full integration was a major undertaking that would unfold over many years, so in addition to launching an extensive series of horizontal activities like developing training standards and devising a system for standardizing currently disparate automated reports, Kirsch also assigned rapidresults teams to quickly put in place several standard operating procedures (SOPs) that cut across the horizontal work streams. The rapidresults teams were focused on the areas he perceived would put the company in the greatest danger of failing to comply with U.S. and European regulations and also on areas where he saw opportunities to generate knowledge that could be applied companywide. There's no science to this approach; it's an iterative process of successive approximation, not a cut-anddried analytical exercise.

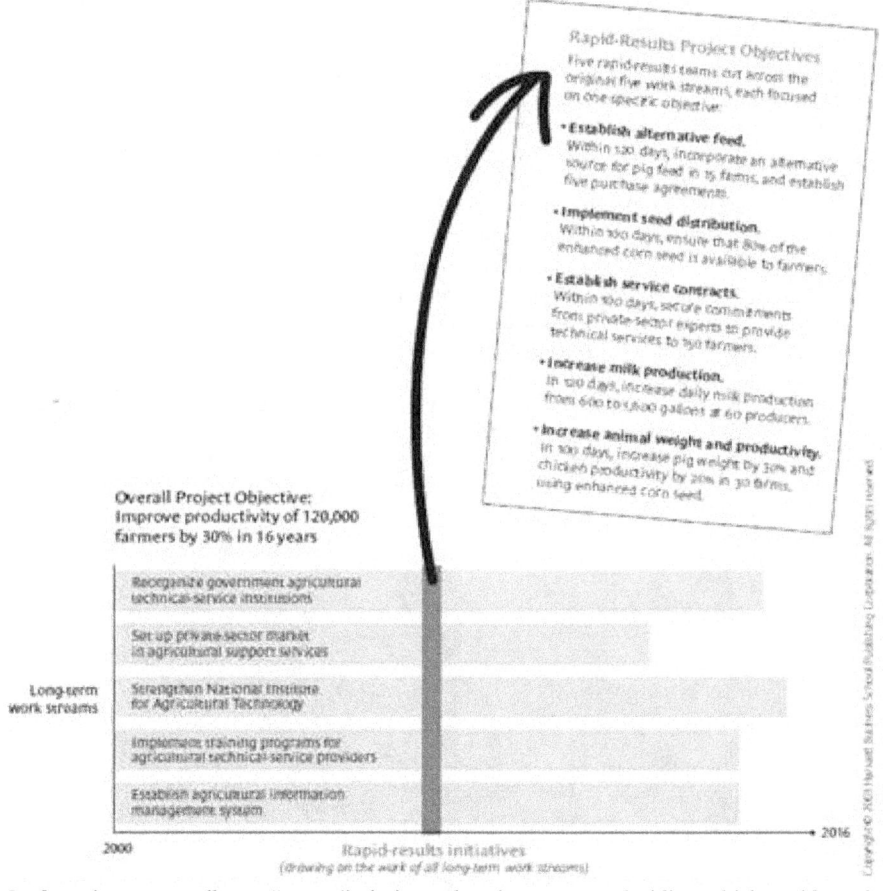

In fact, there are really no "wrong" choices when it comes to deciding which rapid-results initiatives to add to the portfolio. In the context of a large-scale, multiyear, high-stakes effort, each 100-day initiative focused on a targeted result is a relatively low-risk investment. Even if it does not fully realize its goal, the rapid-results initiative will produce valuable lessons and help further illuminate the path to the larger objective. And it will suggest other, and perhaps better-focused, targets for rapid results.

A Call for Humility. Rapid-results initiatives give some new responsibilities to frontline team members while challenging senior leaders to cede control and rethink the way they see themselves. Zurich North America's Gary Kaplan found that the process led him to reflect on his role. "I had to learn to let go: Establishing challenging goals and giving others the space to figure out what it takes to achieve these…did not come naturally to me."

Attempting to achieve complex goals in fastmoving and unpredictable environments is humbling. Few leaders and few organizations have figured out how to do it consistently. We believe that a starting point for greater success is shedding the blueprint model that has implicitly driven executive behavior in the management of major efforts. Managers expect they will be able to identify, plan for, and influence all the variables and players in advance, but they can't. Nobody is that smart or has that clear a crystal ball. They can, however, create an ongoing process of learning and discovery, challenging the people close to the action to produce results—and unleashing the organization's collective knowledge and creativity in pursuit of discovery and achievement.

The World Bank's Project Plan. A project plan typically represents the planned activities as horizontal bars plotted over time. But in most cases, it's very difficult to accurately assess all the activities that will be required to complete a complicated long-term project. We don't know what will fall into the white space between the bars. It's also difficult to know whether these activities can be integrated seamlessly at the end; the teams working in isolation may develop solutions that won't fit together. Rapid-results initiativescut across horizontal activities, focusing on a miniversion of the overall result rather than on a set of activities.

Here is a simplified version of the Nicaragua project described in this article. Each vertical team (depicted as a group by the vertical bar) includes representatives from every horizontal team, which makes the two types of initiatives mutually reinforcing. So, for example, the horizontal work stream labeled "Set up private-sector market in agricultural support services" includes activities like developing a system of coupons to subsidize farmers' purchases. The vertical team establishing service contracts between technical experts and farmers drew on this work, providing the farmers with coupons they could use to buy the technical services. This, in turn, drove competition in the private sector, calling on the work that the people on the horizontal training teams were doing—which led to better services.

CHAPTER 10

The Big Lie of Strategic Planning

A detailed plan may be comforting, but it's not a strategy. by Roger L. Martin

A ll executives know that strategy is important. But almost all also find it scary, because it forces them to confront a future they can only guess at. Worse, actually choosing a strategy entails making decisions that explicitly cut off possibilities and options. An executive may well fear that getting those decisions wrong will wreck his or her career.

The natural reaction is to make the challenge less daunting by turning it into a problem that can be solved with tried and tested tools. That nearly always means spending weeks or even months preparing a comprehensive plan for how the company will invest in existing and new assets and capabilities in order to achieve a target—an increased share of the market, say, or a share in some new one. The plan is typically supported with detailed spreadsheets that project costs and revenue quite far into the future. By the end of the process, everyone feels a lot less scared.

This is a truly terrible way to make strategy. It may be an excellent way to cope with fear of the unknown, but fear and discomfort are an essential part of strategy making. In fact, if you are entirely comfortable with your strategy, there's a strong chance it isn't very good. You're probably stuck in one or more of the traps I'll discuss in this article. You need to be uncomfortable and apprehensive: True strategy is about placing bets and making hard choices. The objective is not to eliminate risk but to increase the odds of success.

In this worldview, managers accept that good strategy is not the product of hours of careful research and modeling that lead to an inevitable and almost perfect conclusion. Instead, it's the result of a simple and quite rough-and-ready process of thinking through what it would take to achieve what you want and then assessing whether it's realistic to try. If executives adopt this definition, then maybe, just maybe, they can keep strategy where it should be: outside the comfort zone.

Comfort Trap 1: Strategic Planning

Virtually every time the word "strategy" is used, it is paired with some form of the word "plan," as in the process of "strategic planning" or the resulting "strategic plan." The subtle slide from strategy to planning occurs because planning is a thoroughly doable and comfortable exercise.

Strategic plans all tend to look pretty much the same. They usually have three major parts. The first is a vision or mission statement that sets out a relatively lofty and aspirational goal. The second is a list of initiatives—such as product launches, geographic expansions, and construction projects—that the organization will carry out in pursuit of the goal. This part of the strategic plan tends to be very organized but also very long. The length of the list is generally constrained only by affordability.

The third element is the conversion of the initiatives into financials. In this way, the plan dovetails nicely with the annual budget. Strategic plans become the budget's descriptive front end, often projecting five years of financials in order to appear "strategic." But management typically commits only to year one; in the context of years two through five, "strategic" actually means "impressionistic."

This exercise arguably makes for more thoughtful and thorough budgets. However, it must not be confused with strategy. Planning typically isn't explicit about what the organization chooses not to do and why. It does not question assumptions. And its dominant logic is affordability; the plan consists of whichever initiatives fit the company's resources.

Mistaking planning for strategy is a common trap. Even board members, who are supposed to be keeping managers honest about strategy, fall into it. They are, after all, primarily current or former managers, who find it safer to supervise planning than to encourage strategic choice. Moreover, Wall Street is more interested in the short-term goals described in plans than in the long-term goals that are the focus of strategy. Analysts pore over plans in order to assess whether companies can meet their quarterly goals.

Comfort Trap 2: Cost-Based Thinking

The focus on planning leads seamlessly to cost-based thinking. Costs lend themselves wonderfully to planning, because by and large they are under the control of the company. For the vast majority of costs, the company plays the role of customer. It decides how many employees to hire, how many square feet of real estate to lease, how many machines to procure, how much advertising to air, and so on. In some cases a company can, like any customer, decide to stop buying a particular good or service, and so even severance or shutdown costs can be under its control. Of course there are exceptions. Government agencies tell companies that they need to remit payroll taxes for each employee and buy a certain amount of compliance services. But the proverbial exceptions prove the rule: Costs imposed on the company by others make up a relatively small fraction of the overall cost picture, and most are derivative of company-controlled costs. (Payroll taxes, for instance, are incurred only when the company decides to hire an employee.)

Costs are comfortable because they can be planned for with relative precision. This is an important and useful exercise. Many companies are damaged or destroyed when they let their costs get out of control. The trouble is that planning-oriented managers tend to apply familiar, comfortable cost-side approaches to the revenue side as well, treating revenue planning as virtually identical to cost planning and as an equal component of the overall plan and budget. All too often, the result is painstaking work to build up revenue plans salesperson by salesperson, product by product, channel by channel, region by region.

But when the planned revenue doesn't show up, managers feel confused and even aggrieved. "What more could we have done?" they wonder. "We spent thousands upon thousands of hours planning."

There's a simple reason why revenue planning doesn't have the same desired result as cost planning. For costs, the company makes the decisions. But for revenue, customers are in charge. Except in the rare case of monopolies, customers can decide of their own free will whether to give revenue to the company, to its competitors, or to no one at all. Companies may fool themselves into thinking that revenue is under their control, but because it is neither knowable nor controllable, planning, budgeting, and forecasting it is an impressionistic exercise.

Of course, shorter-term revenue planning is much easier for companies that have long-term contracts with customers. For example, for business information provider Thomson Reuters, the bulk of its tions. The only variable amount in the revenue plan is the difference between new subscription sales and cancellations at the end of existing contracts. Similarly, if a company has long order backlogs, as Boeing does, it will be able to predict revenue more accurately, although the Boeing Dreamliner tribulations demonstrate that even "firm orders" don't automatically translate into future revenue. Over the longer term, all revenue is controlled by the customer.

The bottom line, therefore, is that the predictability of costs is fundamentally different from the predictability of revenue. Planning can't and won't make revenue magically appear, and the effort you spend creating revenue plans is a distraction from the strategist's much harder job: finding ways to acquire and keep customers.

Comfort Trap 3: Self-Referential Strategy Frameworks

This trap is perhaps the most insidious, because it can snare even managers who, having successfully avoided the planning and cost traps, are trying to build a real strategy. In identifying and articulating a strategy, most executives adopt one of a number of standard frameworks. Unfortunately, two of the most popular ones can lead the unwary user to design a strategy entirely around what the company can control.

In 1978 Henry Mintzberg published an influential article in *Management Science* that introduced *emergent strategy,* a concept he later popularized for the wider nonacademic business audience in his successful 1994 book, *The Rise and Fall of Strategic Planning.* Mintzberg's insight was simple but indeed powerful. He distinguished between *deliberate strategy,* which is intentional, and emergent strategy, which is not based on an original intention but instead consists of the company's responses to a variety of unanticipated events.

Mintzberg's thinking was informed by his observation that managers overestimate their ability to predict the future and to plan for it in a precise and technocratic way. By drawing a distinction between deliberate and emergent strategy, he wanted to encourage managers to watch carefully for changes in their environment and make course corrections in their deliberate strategy accordingly. In addition, he warned against the dangers of sticking to a fixed strategy in the face of substantial changes in the competitive environment.

All of this is eminently sensible advice that every manager would be wise to follow. However, most managers do not. Instead, most use the idea that a strategy emerges as events unfold as a justification for declaring the future to be so unpredictable and volatile that it doesn't make sense to make strategy choices until the future becomes sufficiently clear. Notice how comforting that interpretation is: No longer is there a need to make angst-ridden decisions about unknowable and uncontrollable things.

A little digging into the logic reveals some dangerous flaws in it. If the future is too unpredictable and volatile to make strategic choices, what would lead a manager to believe that it will become significantly less so? And how would that manager recognize the point when predictability is high enough and volatility is low enough to start making choices? Of course the premise is untenable: There won't be a time when anyone can be sure that the future is predictable.

Hence, the concept of emergent strategy has simply become a handy excuse for avoiding difficult strategic choices, for replicating as a "fast follower" the choices that appear to be succeeding for others, and for deflecting any criticism for not setting out in a bold direction. Simply following competitors' choices will never produce a unique or valuable advantage. None of this is what Mintzberg intended, but it is a common outcome of his framework, because it plays into managers' comfort zone.

In 1984, six years after Mintzberg's original article introducing emergent strategy, Birger Wernerfelt wrote "A Resource-Based View of the Firm," which put forth another enthusiastically embraced concept in strategy. But it wasn't until 1990, when C.K. Prahalad and Gary Hamel wrote one of the most widely read HBR articles of all time, "The Core Competence of the Corporation," that Wernerfelt's resource-based view (RBV) of the firm was widely popularized with managers.

RBV holds that the key to a firm's competitive advantage is the possession of valuable, rare, inimitable, and non-substitutable capabilities. This concept became extraordinarily appealing to executives, because it seemed to suggest that strategy was the identification and building of "core competencies," or "strategic capabilities." Note that this conveniently falls within the realm of the knowable and controllable. Any company can build a technical sales force or a software development lab or a distribution network and declare it a core competence.

Executives can comfortably invest in such capabilities and control the entire experience. Within reason, they can guarantee success.

The problem, of course, is that capabilities themselves don't compel a customer to buy. Only those that produce a superior value equation for a particular set of customers can do that. But customers and context are both unknowable and uncontrollable. Many executives prefer to focus on capabilities that can be built—for certain. And if those don't produce success, capricious customers or irrational competitors can take the blame.

Escaping the Traps. It's easy to identify companies that have fallen into these traps. In those companies, boards tend to be highly comfortable with the planners and spend lots of time reviewing and approving their work. Discussion in management and board meetings tends to focus on how to squeeze more profit out of existing revenue rather than how to generate new revenue. The principal metrics concern finance and capabilities; those that deal with customer satisfaction or market share (especially changes in the latter) take the backseat.

How can a company escape those traps? Because the problem is rooted in people's natural aversion to discomfort and fear, the only remedy is to adopt a discipline about strategy making that reconciles you to experiencing some angst. This involves ensuring that the strategy-making process conforms to three basic rules. Keeping to the rules isn't easy—the comfort zone is always alluring—and it won't necessarily result in a successful strategy. But if you can follow them, you will at least be sure that your strategy won't be a bad one.

Rule 1: Keep the strategy statement simple. Focus your energy on the key choices that influence revenue decision makers—that is, customers. They will decide to spend their money with your company if your value proposition is superior to competitors'. Two choices determine success: the where-to-play decision (which specific customers to target) and the how-to-win decision (how to create a compelling value proposition for those customers). If a customer is not in the segment or area where the company chooses to play, she probably won't even become aware of the availability and nature of its offering. If the company does connect with that customer, the how-to-win choice will determine whether she will find the offering's targeted value equation compelling.

If a strategy is about just those two decisions, it won't need to involve the production of long and tedious planning documents. There is no reason why a company's strategy choices can't be summarized in one page with simple words and concepts. Characterizing the key choices as where to play and how to win keeps the discussion grounded and makes it more likely that managers will engage with the strategic challenges the firm faces rather than retreat to their planning comfort zone.

Rule 2: Recognize that strategy is not about perfection. As noted, managers unconsciously feel that strategy should achieve the accuracy and predictive power of cost planning—in other words, it should be nearly perfect. But given that strategy is primarily about revenue rather than cost, perfection is an impossible standard. At its very best, therefore, strategy shortens the odds of a company's bets. Managers must internalize that fact if they are not to be intimidated by the strategy-making process.

For that to happen, boards and regulators need to reinforce rather than undermine the notion that strategy involves a bet. Every time a board asks managers if they are sure about their strategy or regulators make them certify the thoroughness of their strategy decision-making processes, it weakens actual strategy making. As much as boards and regulators may want the world to be knowable and controllable, that's simply not how it works. Until they accept this, they will get planning instead of strategy—and lots of excuses down the line about why the revenue didn't show up.

Rule 3: Make the logic explicit. The only sure way to improve the hit rate of your strategic choices is to test the logic of your thinking: For your choices to make sense, what do you need to believe about customers, about the evolution of your industry, about competition, about your capabilities? It is critical to write down the answers to those questions, because the human mind naturally rewrites history and will declare the world to have unfolded largely as was planned rather than recall how strategic bets were actually made and why. If the logic is recorded and then compared to real events, managers will be able to see quickly when and how the strategy is not producing the desired outcome and will be able to make necessary adjustments—just as Henry Mintzberg envisioned. In addition, by observing with some level of rigor what works and what doesn't, managers will be able to improve their strategy decision making.

As managers apply these rules, their fear of making strategic choices will diminish. That's good—but only up to a point. If a company is completely comfortable with its choices, it's at risk of missing important changes in its environment.

I HAVE argued that planning, cost management, and focusing on capabilities are dangerous traps for the strategy maker. Yet those activities are essential; no company can neglect them. For if it's strategy that compels customers to give the company its revenue, planning, cost control, and capabilities determine whether the revenue can be obtained at a price that is profitable for the company. Human nature being what it is, though, planning and the other activities will always dominate strategy rather than serve it— unless a conscious effort is made to prevent that. If you are comfortable with your company's strategy, chances are you're probably not making that effort.

Giant Opportunities Encourage Bad Strategy. Companies in many industries prefer a small slice of a huge market to a large slice of a small one. The thinking is, of course, that the former promises unlimited growth potential. And there's a certain amount of truth to that. But all too often, the size of the opportunity encourages sloppy strategy making. Why choose where to play or how to win when there's a huge market to conquer? Anybody is a potential customer, so just go out and sell stuff.

But when anyone could be a customer, it is impossible to figure out whom to target and what those people actually want. The results tend to be an offering that is not captivating to anybody and a sales force that doesn't know where to spend its time. This is when crisp strategy making and clear thinking about opportunities are most important.

When you're facing a huge growth opportunity, it is smarter to think sequentially: Determine what piece of the overall market to tackle first and target it precisely and relentlessly. Once you've achieved a dominant position in that segment, expand from there into the next, and so on.

Are You Stuck in the Comfort Zone?

Probably

- You have a large corporate strategic planning group.
- In addition to profit, your most important performance metrics are cost- and capabilities-based.
- Strategy is presented to the board by your strategic planning staff.
- Board members insist on proof that the strategy will succeed before approving it.
- Probably Not
- If you have a corporate strategy group, it is tiny.
- In addition to profit, your most important performance metrics are customer satisfaction and market share.
- Strategy is presented to the board primarily by line executives.
- Board members ask for a thorough description of the risks involved in a strategy before approving it.

The Idea in Brief

The Problem. In an effort to get a handle on strategy, managers spend thousands of hours drawing up detailed plans that project revenue far into the future. These plans may make managers feel good, but all too often they matter very little to performance.

Why It Happens. Strategy making is uncomfortable; it's about taking risks and facing the unknown. Unsurprisingly, managers try to turn it into a comfortable set of activities. But reassurance won't deliver performance.

The Solution. Reconcile yourself to feeling uncomfortable, and follow three rules:

- **Keep it simple.** Capture your strategy in a one-pager that addresses where you will play and how you will win.

- **Don't look for perfection.** Strategy isn't about finding answers. It's about placing bets and shortening odds.

- **Make the logic explicit.** Be clear about what must change for you to achieve your strategic goal.

www.ingramcontent.com/pod-product-compliance
Lightning Source LLC
Chambersburg PA
CBHW070812180526
45168CB00002B/591